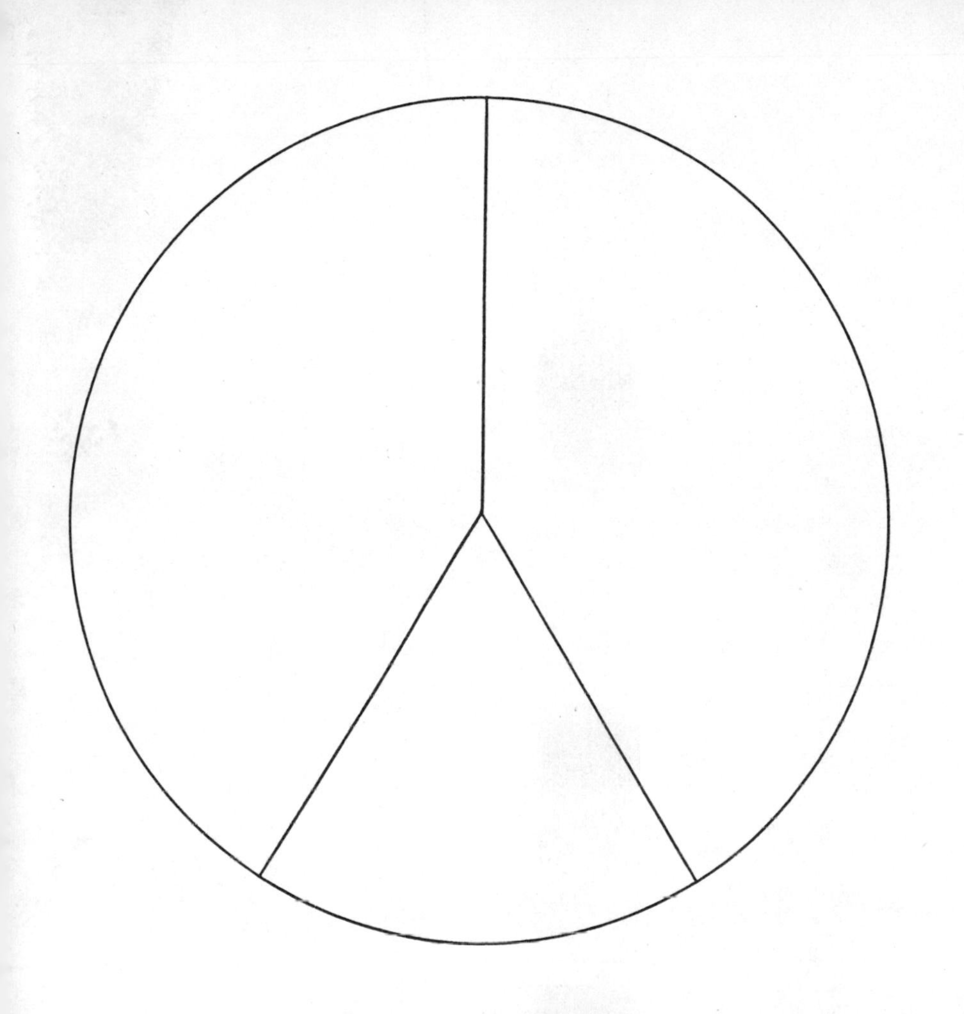

AMEN

The Diary of Rabbi Martin Siegel

EDITED BY MEL ZIEGLER

A MADDICK MANUSCRIPTS BOOK
The World Publishing Company
New York and Cleveland

A Maddick Manuscripts Book
Published by Maddick Manuscripts, Inc.
Distributed by The World Publishing Company
Distributed simultaneously in Canada
by Nelson, Foster & Scott Ltd.
Second Printing—May 1971

Library of Congress catalog card number: 73-142133
Printed in the United States of America

WORLD PUBLISHING
TIMES MIRROR

for Judith

Editor's Note

Two men kept this diary. One was Martin Siegel, husband and father, responsible for keeping up the mortgage payments on a fifteen-room house in an affluent suburb. The other was Rabbi Siegel, the spiritual leader of Temple Sinai, a Reform synagogue in Lawrence, New York, responsible for sermons, bar mitzvahs, weddings, funerals, and an occasional *latke* party.

The diary started off to be the story of Rabbi Siegel, a documentary account of the life of a reasonably typical rabbi, his duties and his difficulties. It was intended to show, through one man, the special nature of his profession.

But halfway through its course, unpredictably, the diary turned into the story of Martin Siegel, the drama of an individual with intensely personal problems.

Ultimately, of course, the two stories fused, and the result is the diary of Rabbi Martin Siegel, the diary of one human being who happens to be a rabbi.

Rabbi Martin Siegel, who is thirty-seven years old, kept this diary for almost a full year, starting late in 1968 and extending deep into 1969. He spoke each day into a tape recorder, describing and analyzing his actions and reactions of the previous twenty-four hours.

For several months afterward, he reviewed the transcripts of his diary. He could see that he had revealed himself to be compassionate yet dispassionate, magnanimous yet resentful, idealistic yet pragmatic, visionary yet blind, committed yet mischievous, self-effacing yet egotistical.

And none of this disturbed him. He was, in fact, delighted by his own frailty.

"I sermonize against the materialism of suburbia," he said, assessing his own words, "while I debate whether to build a $7,000 swimming pool in my backyard. I denounce my Congressman because he doesn't seem to care about the district and I denounce him because he fails to send me complimentary tickets to a luncheon in his honor. I call the synagogue a decadent and dangerous institution while I haggle with my congregation for a raise in pay.

"I suppose some people will see me as pompous, some as petty and some as prophetic. I see myself as human."

In the end, he had the confidence not to censor his spontaneity. He had the courage not to adjust his observations or alter his conclusions. Instead, he amplified, he clarified and he added an epilogue that brought his diary up to date, up into 1970.

Naturally, he is less than perfect in his self-perception. Because there are things he fails to see and things he refuses to see, the diary of Rabbi Martin Siegel is, finally, two stories. One he tells. The other his telling tells.

—MEL ZIEGLER
New York City

Introduction

Why am I a rabbi?

I don't know.

How did I become a rabbi?

I'm not sure.

I had little contact with institutional religion when I was growing up in Brooklyn. My mother considers herself a Reform Jew, but a nonpracticing one; on Friday nights, she prefers Mah-Jongg to services. My father was an Orthodox Jew, and for his sake I attended Hebrew school briefly; then one day a teacher smacked me with a frying pan—I can't remember why—and that was the end of it. For a year before I turned thirteen, I studied with a private tutor, and he prepared me for my bar mitzvah.

The bar mitzvah, the ritualistic coming of age, had no significance for me. My father worried about the religious part, my mother worried about the party part and I worried only about getting it over with. I trembled during the service. I hated the experience.

After my bar mitzvah, I drifted away from the temple. I attended services only occasionally, under pressure from my father.

When I was seventeen, I entered Cornell University, and for some reason, during my first Christmas vacation, I accepted an invitation to speak on college night at my father's Orthodox *shul.* I don't remember exactly my words, but I know I indicated I had no use for a literal interpretation of the Bible. I said I found it hard to believe that Joshua made the sun stand still or that Lot's wife turned to salt. I said that the Bible was a well of myths from which we should draw inspiration and not worry about facts. As I left the synagogue, one of the great men of the congregation stood by the door and screamed at me, "Heretic! Liar!"

At Cornell, I roomed with three classmates who were, like me, very much involved in campus politics. One of them became the president of the student government and another the president of my class. (On a more modest scale, I became president of my fraternity, Phi Sigma Delta, and of the student body of my college, the School of Industrial and Labor Relations.) All three of my roommates were WASPs—white Anglo-Saxon Protestants. My goal at the time was to be accepted in the campus hierarchy, which was very WASPishly oriented, and I tried desperately to fit into their style—dirty white bucks, chino pants, knit ties, the whole *megillah.*

I wasn't consciously rejecting my Jewish identity—and I certainly couldn't have hidden it. After all, my name was Siegel, and I didn't have blond hair, blue eyes or a lanky build to go with the white bucks and chinos. I knew I was a Jew, my roommates—my WASP models—knew I was a Jew and none of us made much of it.

Then one evening two of my roommates—the class president and the student-government president—went out to a party and came home quite drunk. They barged into my room and started berating me about the Jews, how the Jews were this and the Jews were that and I was this and I was that. I've forgotten their precise words—I must have repressed them—but they were insulting and cruel.

My roommates staggered away, and I tried to sleep, but the whole thing kept rolling around in my head. I tried to find some justification for their actions, but I couldn't. I knew that no matter what I thought, no matter how much I had to drink, I never would have said those words to anyone. It wasn't my style. It wasn't my heritage.

I'm always resisting the temptation to say that this one incident caused me to become a rabbi. It didn't. But, coupled with some philosophy courses I was then taking, it did help spur me to a serious study of Judaism and my own Jewishness. I wanted to know what the religion was and what it had to do with the way I was.

The more I learned about Judaism, the more I appreciated it—and the more I realized that too many Jews today were taking this marvelous heritage and distorting it.

By that time, armed with a degree from Hebrew Union College, I had studied myself into the rabbinate.

Suddenly, I was no longer Marty Siegel.

I was the Rabbi.

The Rabbi? I thought. *What is the Rabbi? Who is the Rabbi? What is the Rabbi supposed to be? Why am I the Rabbi?*

Through a decade as a practicing rabbi, first as a chaplain in the Marine Corps, then in Wheeling, West Virginia, and now in Long Island, the questions have never gone away.

—MARTIN SIEGEL
Woodmere, New York

PART ONE

December 12, 1968

The local Jewish community is frightened, and although I do not share their particular fears, I am frightened, too. The community's fear is of the blacks, a growing fear which is feeding hatred, and it is this emerging racism that frightens me. How can Jews, of all people, practice intolerance?

I've sensed this Jewish antagonism toward the blacks for some time, but it has been brought home to me vividly in recent days. The New York *Times* this morning ran a story about the scheduled—and canceled—appearance here of Floyd McKissick, the former national director of the Congress of Racial Equality (CORE). McKissick was supposed to speak here two days ago, but even though he showed up for the engagement and even though I urged him to speak, he did not speak. He did not speak basically because of fear, Jewish fear, and because of racism, Jewish racism. To make the situation worse, McKissick himself added a touch of demagoguery.

The events behind the incident go back four or five months. My congregation, Temple Sinai, and three other local synagogues offer a lecture series called the Five Towns Adult Education Forum. (The so-called Five Towns are Woodmere, in which I live; Lawrence, in which I work; Cedarhurst, Hewlett and Inwood.) During the past summer, a speakers committee, composed of the rabbi and one layman from each congregation, invited McKissick to be one of the forum's 1968–69 speakers and agreed to pay him a fee of $1,000.

There was relatively little debate at the time, but in the past few months Jewish-black relations have been terribly strained by the New York City teachers' strike, revolving around a battle between the predominantly Jewish United Federation of Teachers and the predominantly black Ocean Hill-Brownsville school board, which administers an experimental school district in the black section of Brooklyn. The heart of the dispute is the issue of decentralization, or community control. The blacks, who would like the power both to hire and fire their children's teachers and to redesign the curriculum, favor local community control of the schools; the teachers union, fearful of being splintered, opposes it.

Several weeks ago, Rabbi Edward Sandrow of Temple Beth El, a man who has been sort of an institution in the Five Towns for more than thirty years, called me and said he didn't think we should have McKissick here because McKissick supported community control of the schools.

The United Federation of Teachers has been working to make the term "community control" almost synonymous with "black anti-Semitism." The union has been suggesting, directly and indirectly, that if local communities within New York City were to control their own schools, the result might be vicious reprisals against Jewish teachers in black areas. I don't accept this theory. I believe that community control and black anti-Semitism are two totally different things, linked together only through the efforts of the teachers' union.

"I support community control, too," I told Rabbi Sandrow. "Do you think I shouldn't be here?"

Rabbi Sandrow, I think, was shocked; he is accustomed to

having his own way in the Five Towns. Our disagreement led to several rather heated meetings of the Forum's speakers committee. "I'm not a bigot," one of the lay members of the committee said at the last meeting, "but I don't want any blacks in my community."

I was furious. "People like you are going to create anti-Semitism," I yelled. "People like you are the ones who are really going to hurt the Jewish people."

The man made a conciliatory remark later about excitable rabbis, but I was glad I'd lost my temper. I believe in Judaism, in the wisdom and richness of its traditions, but if he's representative of Judaism, the whole religion has failed.

One of the rabbis at the meeting suggested that, as a compromise, we have Dore Schary, head of the Anti-Defamation League of B'nai B'rith, appear with McKissick and talk on Jewish-black relations. All the rabbis agreed to this proposal, but the lay representatives of three of the congregations—all but mine—refused to go along.

In a final showdown, two congregations felt we should pay McKissick his fee, but not have him speak. One congregation felt we should neither hear nor pay him. My congregation wanted to hear and pay him. Ultimately, for the sake of peace in the community, I accepted the majority view—to pay McKissick, withdraw his invitation and hear Schary alone. I had to relay this decision to McKissick's lecture agent, which was somewhat embarrassing, because McKissick's lecture agent is also the cantor of Temple Sinai.

The cantor is a strange, complex man; he has a fine voice and once dreamed of singing at the Metropolitan Opera, but he never quite made it. Now he runs a lecture bureau and, on weekends, serves as our cantor. He is extremely cynical, both of the community and of the religion. He was upset by the decision to cancel McKissick, but he had mixed feelings because now two of his clients—he is also Schary's agent—were going to receive lecture fees. We contracted to pay Schary $750.

Then, two days ago, the night of the scheduled lecture, I was home eating dinner when I received two telephone calls in quick succession. The first was from the cantor, who told me that McKissick said he had not received his $1,000 check (which had been sent by registered mail) and that he intended to show up to fulfill his contractual obligation. The second was from Rabbi Sandrow. His message: come to Sons of Israel Temple, the site of the lecture, immediately.

When I reached the temple, the other rabbis were frantic. "Marty, Marty, do something," one of them said. "They're here! They're here!" Who's here? I thought. Who's here? The *malach h'mohves*? The angel of death?

I entered the rabbi's office, and there was McKissick in all his blackness, sitting with a few friends from Harlem and with Schary, and they were all talking about the weather and what a nice day it was. I huddled with the other rabbis and, after some discussion, we decided that, since McKissick was there, he should be allowed to speak. "You should be heard," I told him. "You're here. You should speak."

"I've already been told that I cannot speak," McKissick said, "and I'm not going to speak now. I have my pride." I argued with him, trying to persuade him to speak, but he wouldn't change his mind. We shook hands, and he left. Schary stayed and spoke.

The following day—yesterday—the New York *Times* called me and asked me about the incident. Obviously, McKissick, or McKissick's aides, had tipped off the *Times.*

From the reporter's questions, I realized that the story they had was that McKissick had been scheduled to speak, had shown up expecting to speak, had been told he could not speak and had left—which was not precisely the truth. McKissick certainly knew that the invitation had been withdrawn, and I cannot help but feel that he came out to the Five Towns merely to provoke a confrontation, to create an incident which would give him publicity. Otherwise, when we told him he could speak, he would have spoken. I sympathize with his cause and with his aims, but

I think his tactics smacked of demagoguery. My own desire is to improve the relationship between Jews and blacks. I want to prevent confrontations. I want to avoid situations that breed Jewish racism.

Yet, if I am irritated by McKissick's method, I'm grateful to him for pointing up the amount of racism that exists, and is spreading, within the Jewish community. Some people are distressed by the failure of McKissick to speak; some are gloating; and some are completely missing the point. One member of my congregation called me this morning and said, "Rabbi, I want you to know how proud we were to see our rabbi's name in the New York *Times*."

December 13

A small incident tonight showed me the feelings contributing to the fear in the Jewish community. Before our Friday night services, Fred Bobroff, a high-school sophomore whose father is vice-president of our temple, came to me to finish a discussion we had begun the other day, a discussion of the movie, *Gentlemen's Agreement.*

The film had been shown at Lawrence High School, and Fred had been very upset by it because he feared that the anti-Semitic incidents of the film mainly aroused and encouraged anti-Semitism. He told me that he had seen only half the movie, and I had suggested that he see the other half and then talk to me.

"I guess I'm oversensitive," Fred told me tonight, after seeing the rest of the film, which is, of course, basically anti-anti-Semitic. "I've never experienced anti-Semitism myself, but I'm afraid that I might, so when I see even the possibility of it, I try to protect myself."

That's one of the strange things about this community. A lot of people moved here to escape anti-Semitism, to shield their children from anti-Semitism, and now they're so isolated they're twice as frightened of anti-Semitism as they'd be if they had to face it. The specter of *black* anti-Semitism absolutely terrifies most of the people of the Five Towns.

The Five Towns area, on the south shore of Long Island roughly twenty miles east of Manhattan, is one of the choice Jewish communities in the world. It has great affluence and great influence, a concentration of wealth, education, and power. Its sister communities, in spirit, if not in all details, are Shaker Heights, outside Cleveland; Highland Park, outside Chicago; Brookline, outside Boston; Scarsdale, north of Manhattan; and Great Neck, on the north shore of Long Island. It is basically a bedroom community, a haven for commuters, a place where Judaism gets its mail. It is a very impressive mailing address; when I was growing up in Brooklyn, I thought of the Five Towns, more than Israel, as the Promised Land.

Actually, only four of the Five Towns—Woodmere, Lawrence, Cedarhurst and Hewlett—are "Jewish" communities. The fifth, Inwood, is mostly Italian and black; it houses the people who service the other four towns, the domestics, the gardeners and the laborers.

Relatively few non-Jews live in the four core towns, and those that do are almost invisible, especially to a rabbi. Some of them are called "clamdiggers"; they are the descendants of the early settlers of the area. Some are middle-class families who, like their Jewish neighbors, gave up on the city. And some, the extremely wealthy, live in their own plush enclave of large homes and beautiful estates within a section known as Back Lawrence. They have their own country club, and the commuters among them, I'm told, used to ride their own self-segregated Long Island Railroad car into New York City.

The Jews of the Five Towns are basically New Yorkers in everything except residence. They run New York businesses, read New York newspapers, watch New York television, convalesce in New York hospitals, attend New York theaters and eat in New York restaurants.

It is no surprise then that, even though the teachers' strike is taking place in New York City and has no direct impact on the schools of the Five Towns, its side effect—its racist overtone—is being felt here.

There's another, more subtle aspect to this current hysteria. For centuries, the Jews have suffered so much that suffering itself has become almost a sanctified ritual of Judaism. The Jewish experience has been carved out of anguish, and I suspect that the American Jew today, perhaps feeling guilty about his lack of suffering and deprivation, may welcome, at least subconsciously, his imagined black oppressors.

December 14

After services this morning, Bob Mandel, the president of our congregation, talked with me about the cantor. A great deal of opposition to the cantor exists within the congregation, mostly a feeling that he spends too little time here, and his role in the McKissick affair has not helped him any. I imagine that sooner or later he will be replaced.

The cantor is very much like a bull, to look at and to deal with. He is roughly fifty years old, a stocky man, with a face so intense only half of it can smile at any one time. He has a volatile temperament, and there is no pattern to his emotional eruptions. He has served seventeen years as the cantor of Temple Sinai, and I have yet to hear a member of the congregation call him a friend.

There is considerable feeling, probably justified, that the cantor himself urged McKissick to show up for the lecture in order to embarrass the Jewish community of the Five Towns. I can see the flaws in the community, but the cantor seems almost to hate it.

"I'm really a tribal Jew," Bob Mandel told me, "and I'll stand up for my people even when I think they're wrong. I have a certain loyalty, and the cantor doesn't. He's working against the Jewish community."

Bob Mandel is about the same age as the cantor, a bright man, with his master's degree in psychology. He's in the import-export business, and he deals largely with South American firms. Since he seems quite interested in South American politics, I'm always kidding him about working for the CIA. He was one of the first people I met from this congregation.

In 1966, after five years in Wheeling, West Virginia, I felt that it was time for me to move on to another congregation. I entered my name with the rabbinical placement office in New York. "Your record's fine," the office informed me. "We can recommend you for any job that's available—in your category."

It's a real rabbinical civil service. On the basis of size, salary and a few other things, congregations are rated A, B, C, and D. Rabbis, too, are rated A, B, C, and D, strictly on the basis of how many years they've been out of rabbinical school. It has nothing to do with ability, thank God, considering who'd be doing the rating. I was rated C, and among the temples then looking for a rabbi was Temple Sinai, also rated C; we were matched, as if by a computer dating service. I went to the Five Towns and sat through a formal but reasonable interview with eight people huddled around a conference table—the pulpit committee, a lovely name—and then Mandel and two other Temple Sinai board members came to Wheeling to examine the beast in his natural habitat. Apparently, I survived the examination. I jumped from Wheeling, the Pony League of Judaism, up to the big leagues.

December 15

We had a heavy snow last night, canceling a meeting of our religious-school faculty today, canceling a Hanukkah *latke* party, canceling a talk I was supposed to give to a Catholic group in Brooklyn. I was grateful for a day of rest, a chance to work on a book review, a chance to collect myself and get organized for the week ahead.

The snow let up tonight, and the streets were clear enough for me to drive to dinner at my uncle's temple in Belle Harbor, a nearby community. I enjoyed the opportunity to go to a temple and not be a public figure and not give a speech, merely to relax. We had a rather heavy meal, and it lay on my stomach for a long time, but I guess that's one of the prices we pay for being Jewish.

December 16

Albert Shanker, the president of the United Federation of Teachers in New York, leader of the fight against decentralization of the schools, came to the Five Towns today. He spoke at Temple Beth Sholem, an Orthodox synagogue just down the street from Sinai. I went to the speech mostly to listen, to ask a few questions, to show that there are Jews who favor decentralization.

Shanker arrived late, so while we waited for him, Rabbi Gilbert Klaperman of Beth Sholem, the host, invited me to share the platform with him and say a few words. Naturally, I couldn't resist the temptation. Rabbi Klaperman is a pleasant, intelligent man and president of the New York Board of Rabbis, the largest rabbinical organization in the metropolitan area. He outlined the Board of Rabbis' position in the decentralization dispute. He mentioned that the group generally doubted the value of decentralization and, also, worried about increasing anti-Semitism among the blacks.

I argued that the UFT itself had done more to foment anti-Semitism than any other group. A relative handful of anti-Semitic blacks had put out a relatively small amount of viciously anti-Semitic material, and the union had produced thousands of copies of this literature and had distributed it far more widely than the blacks could ever have done themselves. I suggested that the UFT was seeking to capitalize upon fears of anti-Semitism to solidify its own position, that the UFT was deliberately turning the decentralization dispute into a battle between blacks and Jews.

Just as I was saying this, Albert Shanker came in. The audience, many teachers, many fearful Jews, had not taken well to what I said. They warmed to Shanker quickly. He is an intelligent man, well informed on educational matters, but I feel intuitively that, whether he realizes it or not, he is opposed to the blacks, as well as to decentralization. Many of the people in the audience told Shanker how wonderful they thought he was, how they respected him for standing up to the outrageous demands of the black community. So much of the Jewish community seems truly racist. They're afraid. They have this post-Auschwitz feeling that everybody is persecuting them. They see the black man as a persecutor. They want to hear that the black man is bad and that the black man is out to get them, and Shanker, in a nice polite way, tells them that.

Shanker's hypocrisy, wrapping racism inside an almost holy crusade, infuriated me. I got up and told him, with some overstatement, that he was probably the most dangerous man in Jewish history for instigating this war between the Jews and the blacks, that he was worse than the oppressors of the Jewish people because he was bringing out their worst instincts. He's a dangerous, dangerous man. He is corrupting the values of Judaism.

I had a little support. I had helped bring to the meeting a few young people from the Five Towns who work in the Ocean Hill–Brownsville school district, young Jewish people who are working for decentralization, and they argued with Shanker that the Ocean Hill–Brownsville project was succeeding, that decentralization was the educational hope for these black people.

Much of the audience hated me, actually hated me, for what I said. "Rabbi," one man said, as I left, "we can't let these niggers take everything away from us. We've got to fight them. If you don't fight them, there's something wrong with you."

"If that's your attitude," I said, "you're going to make certain that there is a terrible confrontation, that your house is going to be burned down and my house is going to be burned down."

"I don't care," he said. "I'm going to fight these niggers."

I had no diplomacy left. "Just give me your name and your address," I said, "and I'll give it to them and I'll see that your house is put to the match first—because you deserve it!"

"What kind of rabbi are you?" he said. "You're a disgrace to our people. I'm going to call your congregation."

I left Beth Sholem shaking with anger, my ears burning, "Nigger lover, nigger lover."

But a few people walked over and congratulated me, and

one woman came up to me and said, "I'm so proud of you, Rabbi," and kissed me, and it made my fury seem worthwhile.

December 17

The day certainly started on a cosmic note. The phone rang at 9:30 A.M., and the long-distance caller asked me, "What is the Jewish position on immortality?"

The caller was a member of my former congregation in Wheeling, and he told me that he was going to dinner with the present rabbi and that he wanted to be able to discuss the subject of immortality intelligently with him.

I explained that while Judaism allowed a great deal of flexibility on the subject—and that nobody I knew could prove anything one way or the other—the emphasis generally was on doing good deeds in this life and that they might lead to some kind of ultimate destiny. I told him that we don't put much emphasis on the survival of the ego, none on hell and very little on heaven. The caller said that he personally felt there should be some idea of heaven, and I told him that was fine, that was perfectly all right with me.

The day ended on a far more practical note. My congregation is planning to build a new temple, and construction bids were supposed to be in yesterday. I called Bob Mandel tonight to ask him what had happened, and he told me he hadn't seen the bids yet.

I'm ambivalent about this proposed new building, even though I'm convinced we need more space. Temple Sinai was founded eighteen years ago by people who broke away from Temple Israel, the largest Reform synagogue in the Five Towns, and now we have some 300 families in our congregation. We've simply outgrown our rather dilapidated facilities. Still, I hesitate, because I feel the last thing Judaism needs now is another glittering supersanctuary, designed by a new Frank Lloyd Wright, decorated by a new Michelangelo and prayed in by robots.

Our Five Towns rival, Temple Israel, is symbolized to me by its new ballroom. I've heard that the ballroom, along with some other additions to the building, cost something around $1 million. God knows it has every conceivable luxury—special wood paneling, incredible crystal chandeliers, the most garish adornments. It can seat 700 people comfortably and a bar mitzvah there, offering everything from matzoh-ball soup to nuts. can cost between $5,000 and $15,000. I find it an abomination.

But it is hardly unique. All over the United States, Jews are building monuments to themselves with roughly the same speed and taste as Colonel Sanders putting up his fried-chicken stands.

I don't really want to be in the Judaism franchise business. I suspect that if we don't get our new building, some of our members, those who are looking mostly for a service station where they can fill up with religion and dinner parties, will defect to Temple Israel. The membership fees are about the same in the two synagogues, and I've actually heard prospective members say, "Why should I buy a Ford when I can get a Cadillac for the same price?" I wouldn't miss these comparison shoppers.

There's another reason I'm skeptical about the new building. I have a three-year contract which expires in June, 1970, and when we start discussing renewal next fall, I'm going to be asking for a considerable increase in salary. I want them to be able to afford me, and with a huge mortgage, there won't be much left for anything else. I don't want to be devoured by a gigantic monster of a building.

I really don't need any more money. My current salary is $17,000 a year, and in addition, I make extra money teaching at a local academy, conducting summer institutes and presiding at weddings and funerals, all of which, with some investments, brings my annual income at present to close to $25,000. The reason I will demand a salary increase is because in this community one's ability is measured by the amount of money he makes. Some people here would feel a greater sense of communication with God if their rabbi made an extra $10,000 a year. Then again, since my salary is strictly a private matter, maybe I want the increase to reassure myself that I'm what the congregation really wants, not just what they can afford.

December 18

Bob Mandel heard about my confrontation the other night with Shanker. He called me this morning and told me he feared I might get myself in a position where I would be blocked off from the white community. He wasn't urging me to turn my back on the blacks; he just wanted me to be more careful.

Mandel's own background is leftist—the American Students Union, the SDS of its day—and he said he's terribly distressed to see his older son, a student at Cornell, has turned conservative. His son is totally opposed to black student militancy at Cornell. Bob Mandel himself is sort of a symbol of what's happening to the liberal Jew. His instincts are good, yet he has become cautious; he wants to be certain that neither I nor the temple become too closely linked to a radical cause. To a greater or lesser extent, everyone is frightened.

In the afternoon I went to New York City with the principal of our religious school, Mrs. Arthur Brackman, to meet with the education staff of the Union of American Hebrew Congregations. We've made a number of basic changes in the curriculum of our religious school, and the UAHC has become interested in our program.

Kids today look upon Judaism as, at best, a fairly interesting anachronism. To them, religious school makes Judaism look like the dead hand of the past; there is rarely a suggestion that it has any relevance to their lives.

We've tried to change the approach. We don't ask the kids what hero did this or what hero did that, but we do ask: What is a hero? How does one become a hero? Who are the heroes of today? Why do we even need heroes? We try to be relevant.

The Union of American Hebrew Congregations told us today that they'd designated our school a pilot school for the entire country. Our experiments will be the basis for curriculum changes in all Reform synagogues. It's a very encouraging sign to me, an indication that Judaism may be starting to move in a progressive direction.

My in-laws arrived this evening from Charleston, South Carolina, and they'll probably stay with me and my wife, Judith, for at least a week or two. My father-in-law, Thomas Tobias, is a descendant of one of the most distinguished early Jewish families in the United States; his ancestors arrived in Charleston some two hundred and fifty years ago. He's deeply interested in American Jewish history, and recently, for his work in the field, his published articles, and his collected archives, he received an honorary degree from my alma mater, Hebrew Union College. My mother-in-law, born a Presbyterian, is a convert to Judaism, and, like many converts, she takes her Judaism very seriously. They hadn't seen our daughter, Sally, who will be two in a few weeks, in about six months, and they enjoyed playing with her. We enjoyed watching them almost as much.

December 19

I conducted a funeral this morning and afterward, during the traditional meal of consolation, a woman who is a member of Temple Israel came up to me. "Rabbi," she said, "what do you think of the new ballroom at *our* temple?"

"I think," I said, "that it is morally and esthetically grotesque."

The woman gave me an icy look. "When your salary is as large as our Rabbi's," she said, "then you'll be able to talk."

December 20

The Jews and the birds are in Florida, and things are very quiet in the community. Tonight we had a lightly attended service commemorating the first night of Hanukkah.

December 21

I conducted a wedding ceremony tonight at a banquet hall in eastern Long Island that normally caters to Gentiles. I recited the traditional prayers among holly wreaths, mistletoe, and other symbols of the Christmas season.

Still, the manager of the place tried his best to Judaize the facilities. For example, he made a big point of the fact that the wine was not only perfectly kosher, but was also sealed for my inspection. Only I could break the seal. I suppose he thought we were having a Jewish communion.

Later, during the ceremony of cutting the bread, the manager brought out a bowl of water. He must have heard that it is an ancient Jewish ritual, rarely practiced today, to preface certain occasions by washing. The groom didn't know anything about the ritual. But he dipped his hands in the water, then wiped them on his pants.

In one respect, anyway, the wedding was authentically Jewish. One of the bride's relatives had not arrived by the time we were scheduled to begin the ceremony. Her family loudly insisted on waiting; the groom's loudly insisted on starting. The caterer insisted that if we didn't start, the food would be ruined. I was called on to mediate, and I ruled, in the best tradition of King Solomon and Irving Berlin, that the ceremony must go on.

The moment I made my decision, of course, the disputed relative showed up.

It was a fairly typical Long Island wedding, and every now and then during the dancing following the ceremony, the band stopped playing the *hora* and broke into the theme song of these affairs: "Sit down, sit down, the next course is served. Sit down, sit down, the next course is served."

As I was leaving, the manager of the banquet hall gave me his card and told me he was "trying to get a little deeper into the Jewish market."

December 22

Temple Sinai and Temple Israel co-sponsored a college breakfast today, and in the discussion that followed, the students mirrored the views of their parents on the blacks. Clearly, just by their attendance at a synagogue function, these young people were not the campus radicals.

They had no sympathy for the blacks. One after another, they took the floor to tell what the blacks had done to "try and take control" on their campuses. A coed from the University of Chicago praised the Chicago police as "wonderful, because they protect me." A Columbia student said that the police had been provoked on his campus, that the radicals had no legitimate demands and that, if they did, the vice-president's door was always open. One student, predicting a violent confrontation, urged the others to take up arms to be ready for the blacks.

Is this our next generation of Jews? I wondered.

December 23

I attended a meeting today of a group of clergymen who are planning to lobby in Albany for favorable legislative action on school decentralization. There were several priests and several ministers on hand.

I was the only rabbi.

In the evening, I got a call from a friend who's been working with the blacks in Inwood. He said that the blacks were demanding a school holiday on Martin Luther King's birthday next month. The school administration is all upset because a group of liberal white students also want to stay out of school that day.

I don't really see what the problem is. In the Five Towns, none of the black students has to go to school on his Jewish holidays. Why not let everyone off on Dr. King's birthday?

December 24

An old high-school friend, Henry Cohen, who's now a history professor at Long Beach State College in California, came to dinner tonight. When we were teen-agers, I distinctly remember he had no use for religion.

About two years ago, Henry heard of a professor at his campus who had been beaten up by a group of policemen. Even though he did not know the man, Henry became involved and even traveled to Washington to pursue the matter; finally, the police were brought up on federal charges of violating the civil rights of the professor.

I told Henry that he had done a very Jewish thing. It was my feeling that his concern for justice was an unmistakable residual from his Jewish background.

In this sense, he is typical of many Jews today who are unconsciously fulfilling the teachings of the Jewish religion in their community lives, even though they have no association with official Judaism. Official Judaism, I'm afraid, is more concerned with itself these days than with such things as matters of justice. Today it is not uncommon for the secularized, nonaffiliated, nonreligious Jew, like Henry, to do what Jewish institutions should be doing if they weren't so preoccupied with preserving themselves.

December 25

Today is Christmas, a difficult day for Jews, because, although they feel an identification with the lights, the joy, and the humanity, they really can't participate in the holiday. Jews who buy Christmas trees feel slightly guilty. In recent years, there has been a conscious effort to elevate Hanukkah to separate-but-equal status, but Jews still find it a disappointing substitute.

I sense they would like to have Christmas instead.

Our dog unexpectedly gave birth to six puppies this afternoon. We tried not to make too much of the fact that the puppies arrived this particular day.

December 26

A doctor who is a former member of our congregation and a friend of Abram Vossen Goodman, our rabbi emeritus, asked Rabbi Goodman to conduct the funeral of his father today. As a matter of protocol, my predecessor insisted that, as the incumbent rabbi, I participate in the funeral with him.

Rabbi Goodman makes a point of treating me kindly and politely, but I would rather he had spared me the courtesy this time. I don't care much for funerals. I view them as an opportunity to be of service, but my job demands that I handle so many of them—too often for persons I never knew—that I sometimes feel like a machine producing the necessary rites for departure.

December 27

In my sermon tonight, I dealt with the need for rethinking the role of the synagogue, a topic inspired by our plans for a new building. I called the synagogue a grotesque institution because it mainly serves the purpose of safeguarding antique forms and preserving itself while the essence of religion strays elsewhere. "You know, Dad," I heard the son of another rabbi say to his father recently, "you really ought to get into another field. There's no future in rabbinical work. You're the custodian of a museum."

A synagogue, I said tonight, should exist to foster communication between man and man and, hopefully, between man and God, and this requires that we *be* a community before we worry about housing ourselves as one. If we were a real community, I pointed out, a building would be of little concern; a new structure will only make us more pretty, not less empty.

As a practical matter, I realize that the new building is almost a certainty, so, after I'd scolded the congregation for the concept, I urged that the building be kept modest. I think an unpretentious building is vital for the future of this congregation.

Because our present building is, to be very kind, unpretentious, we have benefited from a reverse snob appeal. The generally rundown condition of our quarters has discouraged people whose attachment is mainly to facade; I'd hate to see our new building so sumptuous that these people will be tempted to join us. I prefer instead the sort of people we now attract, the sort of people who helped found Temple Sinai.

Before World War II, Temple Israel was the only Reform congregation in the Five Towns, and its leading members were wealthy Jews, mostly of German descent, who had long been settled in the community. After the war, as the economy began to boom, a different kind of Jew began moving into the Five Towns, from Brooklyn, from Manhattan, from the Bronx, people who were first beginning to taste affluence, many of them with an Eastern European heritage.

The newcomers joined Temple Israel and then, as they began to press for and take over the leadership, their relations with the earlier members grew extremely bitter. I'm not certain of all the details, but the conflict eventually centered around the rabbi, a strong-willed man named Judah Cahn.

Rabbi Cahn had been at Temple Israel before the newcomers arrived, but, for some reason, the old-liners wanted him fired, and the newcomers wanted to retain him. The dispute was so emotional, so much a test of power, that families actually divided over the issue, and friendships completely dissolved. There are to this day people who will not talk to one another because of the fight.

When the congregation finally met and voted to retain Rabbi Cahn, the president and the majority of the board resigned and founded Temple Sinai. The splinter group, largely the established German Jews of the area, was built around people who tended to underplay their wealth, but not their power. They were intelligent, charitable—and domineering.

The people who now seem to dominate Temple Israel are, in large part, the type who have become too common in Jewish suburbia—self-made men who flaunt their wealth a little too much, painted ladies with dyed hair who drive their Cadillacs too fast.

Temple Israel today is a supercongregation, with 1,200 families to the 300 of Temple Sinai. And two ballrooms to none.

After the services tonight, my wife Judith and I went out for an ice cream soda with a couple who are members of Temple Israel. The couple said they were unhappy because their temple was becoming more and more a playground for the nouveau riche who have no genuine religious feeling.

The conversation reaffirmed my feeling. I want us to build a synagogue, not a playground.

December 28

After services this morning, the cantor cross-examined me about what my predecessor, Rabbi Goodman, thinks of him. Rabbi Goodman doesn't like the cantor, but I didn't bother going into details. "On occasion," I told the cantor, "he's had some things to say about you."

This set him off.

"I'm the nigger here," he said, "and I've been the nigger of this congregation for more than fifteen years."

The cantor is absolutely convinced that everyone is plotting against him—including me. (He has asked me to promise not to use his name in my diary, and, rather than argue with him, I've agreed.)

The fact is that there actually is a group plotting against the cantor. In his seventeen years with the synagogue, his bitterness and bluntness—he refers to members of the congregation as "grown-up Boy Scouts" and "secret Nazis"—have alienated many people.

I keep urging him to become a part of the community, but he always rejects my overtures. He obviously resents the fact that, even though I'm younger, I am, in a way, his boss. Also, I earn a larger salary.

He gets $8,500 a year for one morning and one evening a week, plus a few holidays, but he doesn't think it's enough. He told me today that because he's underpaid he has to drive an inadequate automobile and, as a result, his car has twice spun off the highway, nearly killing his family. This is the logic of utter frustration.

January 3

My sermon tonight was prompted by the space spectacular last week, by the astronauts circling the moon in preparation for a landing later this year. I told the congregation that man, with his earthbound preoccupations of self and accomplishment, seems to have lost sight of his own unimportance. I believe that going to the moon will serve to break down this egocentricity, man's tendency to see himself as the maker of all value, the center of all truth. As he gets the opportunity to look at himself from outer space, he will be able to comprehend physically that he is not so unique, that he is only a speck in a timeless, endless experience.

It was one of my better sermons.

January 4

I was asked to play Solomon again today. Two young people who are planning to be married came to me, with their parents, and with a question: Should the wedding be kosher?

The boy's parents said they maintain a kosher home and they would prefer a kosher wedding. The girl's parents said they do not keep a kosher home and they oppose a kosher wedding. Both sides agreed to abide by my momentous decision.

Of all the people involved, I know only the girl's parents, who are distant relatives of mine. They are, I've found, socially conscious people who live beyond their means; I suppose they object to a kosher wedding because it would cost more without offering any compensating status.

It was the girl's mother who had suggested that I would be an impartial judge—even though she knew that I do not maintain a kosher home myself, that I believe the dietary laws, useful in Biblical times, have little point today.

I listened to both sides for two hours, then ruled that the wedding should be kosher, simply because I felt it meant more to the one couple to have it than it did to the other couple not to have it.

The young lady's mother called this evening to inform me that another rabbi would be performing the wedding ceremony.

January 6

In recent weeks, there has been a rash of synagogue fires in the New York area, and although no one has any proof, a good number of Jews suspect that the arsonists are black. Inevitably, the fear of black anti-Semitism is feeding rumors of black anti-Semitism.

The Brooklyn Board of Rabbis is among the few groups trying to keep communication open between Jews and blacks, and today I went to one of their meetings to hear the Reverend Herbert Oliver, the chairman of the governing board of the Ocean Hill–Brownsville school district.

The Brooklyn rabbis showed Reverend Oliver copies of an editorial in the *Afro-American Teachers Forum*, published by black teachers in New York, accusing the Jewish establishment of keeping down the blacks—socially, economically, and politically. Jews, the editorial charged, are entrenched in the city's power structure and will not give way to let the blacks have their share of power.

The rabbis said they took this as an allusion to Albert Shanker, the president of the teachers union, and they resented the use of Shanker to justify anti-Jewish sentiments. "He's a Jew, yes," one rabbi said, "but he is not Jewish."

Another rabbi said that he and a group of his colleagues had visited Shanker in prison during Hanukkah, when the union leader was serving a sentence for leading an illegal strike. The rabbis brought Shanker Hanukkah candles and offered to say prayers with him.

"The only thing I want from you," Shanker supposedly told the rabbis, "is to get me out of here so I can get my children their Christmas presents."

I don't know whether the story is totally true or not, but I do know that Shanker—more than the *Afro-American Teachers Forum*—is driving a wedge between Jews and blacks.

When I got home tonight, I learned that one hundred and twenty students, all but twenty of them black, had walked out of Lawrence High School today after presenting the school administration with a list of demands.

The demands themselves are moderate—one is that a portrait of Martin Luther King be hung in the school's foyer next to the portrait of John F. Kennedy—but I think the fact that they walked out is more significant than what they walked out for.

The black students are trying to force recognition of the authenticity of their purpose. They want their grievances treated seriously and swiftly. More than anything else, I suspect, they are distressed by the rather patronizing attitude of the superintendent of schools, a man given to hiding within channels and committees, tactics which the students consider deliberate delay.

The superintendent is meeting tomorrow morning with a group of parents, and I will be there, to add my opinions.

January 7

At the meeting this morning, the superintendent of schools wasted about two hours trying to justify his delaying tactics. "You teach about revolution in your schools," I told him. "Now you have one on your hands."

Finally, the administration agreed to start recruiting more black teachers and guidance counselors, to recognize the black youth groups and to put up a portrait of Martin Luther King.

I felt it was, at least, a start. And I felt, too, that the black students learned more from this confrontation than they had from six months in the classroom.

January 8

I met this afternoon with my confirmation class, a coed group of tenth-graders who are preparing for a ceremony in which they will finally commit themselves to Judaism. Students in our congregation are confirmed at the end of their tenth and last required year of religious school.

In early Reform Judaism, confirmation was a substitute for the bar mitzvah, but now we have both. Since confirmation is a rather stylish thing these days, the attendance at these classes is reasonably faithful. I attempt to keep the discussion relevant—perhaps too relevant—and today we spent much of the time talking about the dispute at Lawrence High School.

While most of the students supported or sympathized with the blacks' position, a number of them did not. The students who opposed the strike made a large point about how the blacks were beating up the Jews in school, a rather ludicrous turn of events if true, because the Jews outnumber the blacks by a ratio of at least sixteen to one. I asked these students why they didn't defend themselves.

They had no answers. But I did.

Among the worst of their inclinations, Jews tend to conjure up the charge of anti-Semitism to meet all their crises. It is a convenient defense, through which they justify themselves and discredit the opposition, all in one swift loosening of the tongue.

"Well, should we fight back?" asked one of the students.

"I would like to see a world where all opposing groups were reconciliated," I said, "but that doesn't seem to be man's nature. The world is made up of contending powers and forces, and we all have to be tough to operate in it. In this sense, our goal must be to coalesce our own power as a means of diminishing the opposition's."

"But should we fight back?" the student persisted.

"If in fact the Jews are getting knocked around at the high school," I said, "there is a more creative way to respond than this genteel pacifism of dismissing the brutes as anti-Semitic. And—no—it is not by 'fighting back.' "

I left it at that. I was not about to outline a strategy for them.

January 9

When I agreed to come to Temple Sinai, no one told me about the ritual committee, a group inclined to consume hours haggling over the minutiae of the religious service. The name has since been changed to the committee on worship, but while it has begun to broaden its outlook, I still frequently find myself at odds with it.

Tonight, at its regular meeting, the committee on worship tackled among other things such momentous topics as how the rabbi should announce the number of the page he is reading, the proper mode of dress for people sitting on the pulpit, and who should read what portion and when.

One of my more ambitious goals here has been to nudge this committee into a broader concern for religious worship. Something happened toward the end of the meeting tonight which represented a great breakthrough to me.

One of the members announced that he felt that experimentation was at the heart of discovering religious forms which meant something to people, and that therefore experimentation in the service was in order. I could have been listening to a tape recording of myself.

As if they were dealing with just another matter of trivia, the committee agreed that experimentation was in order. I left the meeting with instructions to be more explicit in reading page numbers and to experiment in the service.

January 10

I attended another meeting today of a group of clergymen supporting community control of the Ocean Hill–Brownsville school district, and, once again, I was the only Jew present.

It is terribly frustrating—and revealing. For so long, Jews have been the leading champions of liberal causes in the New York area, and I realize now that our motivation hasn't been exactly one hundred percent pure: the causes have been ones from which we Jews ourselves would be most likely to benefit.

Those of us few Jews working for community control now find ourselves in the position of pioneering a new kind of Judaism—Judaism without tribalism.

And, of course, this does not make for happy relations within the tribe. Bitter reaction from my community, and my own congregation, is beginning to make itself felt. I am becoming a convenient target for the people who disagree with me. My words are being distorted, my actions misreported.

At a recent Board of Education meeting, for instance, I said that if the superintendent of schools could not develop an effective relationship with the blacks, he should be replaced. The rumor going around the community is that I said the superintendent should be fired summarily. In another incident, the night of my discussion with Shanker, when a woman rose to charge that the Jews of Lawrence had been threatened with extinction if they did not yield to the demand of hiring a black assistant principal, I told the woman that this was not true, that the "threatening" letter was available and she should read it because it was considerably less militant. Word in the community now has it that I called the woman a liar. I am also being accused of supporting General De Gaulle's position on limited arms shipments to Israel—a subject on which I have never uttered a word, publicly or privately.

The teen-agers of our congregation wrote and conducted our service tonight. The essence of what they said is that people don't listen to one another. Parents don't listen to children, children don't listen to parents, whites don't listen to blacks and blacks don't listen to whites. One of the youths gave a sermon accusing the adult generation of apathy on everything from Biafra to Vietnam.

On the whole, the service was a diligent effort to plead with people to communicate with one another, a very enriching event replete with a number of folk songs. One youth came to the service in a sport shirt. Most of the congregation approved of the experimental service, but several people were obviously unhappy. One woman came up to me afterward and said, "Rabbi, what kind of thing is that? No coat and tie?"

She must have been watching the service, but I wonder if she heard a word.

January 11

At a reception for the bar mitzvah boy after today's service, I was introduced to a man who said he was in the vending-machine business. His relatives later hinted he was a racketeer. "Rabbi," he said, "I want to tell you something. Black people—they're nothing. You can't give them anything, because whatever you give them, they'll destroy. If it was up to me, Rabbi, I would stand there with a gun and shoot ever nigger down. I hate them, Rabbi; I hate every single one of them."

This fit of overt racism was a bit embarrassing to some of the other people who were standing in our cluster. I do, however, think that this man represents a very real point of view among Jews. He just expresses it more honestly.

Another member of my congregation, reacting to last night's youth service, told me how my services were often a bridge between generations. "We need you very much and we appreciate what you've done," he said, "but if you don't moderate your views, I'm afraid people won't listen to you."

Another straw in the wind. It indicates, I feel, the beginning of a concerted campaign by some people to get rid of me, or at least embarrass me and make things more difficult.

January 14

Rabbi Lloyd Tannenbaum of Huntington, Long Island, one of the few rabbis working, like me, for school decentralization, called me early this morning. His congregation has fired him. He was too outspoken.

With my own contract expiring next year, an event like this could portend disaster. It is not inconceivable that the board of Temple Sinai will turn on me. It is a possibility I must think seriously about.

Even though I am not, to my thinking, purposely being disruptive, or even provocative, I am doing things which must be done and saying things which must be said. I believe in greater self-destiny for the black people; they must be allowed to achieve their own way. If I had to choose between my work for this cause and being retained by my congregation, I would have to give up the congregation.

But I hope that I won't have to make the choice.

An acquaintance in the community called this evening and invited me to attend a meeting of middle-aged left-wingers. He mentioned that an old friend of his was soon to be released from jail—Morton Sobel, who was convicted of espionage some two decades ago. Sobel was convicted with the Rosenbergs; they were executed, and he was sent to prison.

I was in my teens when the Rosenbergs and Sobel were convicted, and I remember that, at the time, I considered the people working for their acquittal, or their release, to be Communists—or at least extreme leftists trying to undermine the nation. I wouldn't have anything to do with them.

Now these people are aging liberals, and I am, on many issues, considerably to the left of them. It's strange. I am making a good income these days, I have several investments, I have a comfortable home in the suburbs—everything which should dictate a more conservative approach to life. And, yet, the more I collect in material terms, the more I am concerned for those who have too little. I have been radicalized.

January 15

Today would have been Martin Luther King's fortieth birthday, and I participated in two memorial services for him. It is a Christian tradition, extending to Christ and Christmas, to honor people on the day of their birth. If Dr. King had been a Jew, we would memorialize his death, not his birth. The Jewish tradition is to remember a life fulfilled, rather than a life begun.

The first service today took place at Woodmere Academy, an expensive private school—I teach there one afternoon a week—brimming with students who talk about going to Spain the way I talk about going across the street. Surprisingly, some of them are able to remain decent human beings, relatively untarnished by opulence, with a real concern for social justice. Still, their radicalism tends to be the comfortable, convenient brand.

During the memorial service today, I had the depressing feeling that the whole arrangement was more a matter of liberal etiquette than of any sincere conviction. And as the service ended, with the singing of "We Shall Overcome," in the sweet, quiet moment that followed, a faculty member took the microphone to announce, "All those students who are taking Typing II please report to Room 128 next Monday."

The second service was conducted by black people at a black church. Black congregations are so wonderfully responsive. The service was long—obviously, blacks have gotten used to staying in church for long periods, perhaps out of the Southern tradition, where it was the only decent place they could go—and the speeches were interspersed with singing. My speech on this occasion was very important to me, because I said something publicly which I had never said before. A year ago, when Dr. King was killed, a service was held at this same church, a service in which the mournful liturgy mixed with the police sirens outside. At that time I made a private vow to myself. Martin Luther King was so young and gifted and he stood for something very important, something representing justice for the black man and peace for society. I vowed then that I would carry on his goals.

I told this black congregation of that vow today. It made me feel good.

Incidentally, all the black students stayed home from Lawrence High School today, and so did some whites, even though it wasn't an official school holiday, like Rosh Hashanah and Washington's Birthday.

In the evening I met privately with Al Vorspan, a member of my congregation's social action committee and, more important, the national director for social action for Reform Judaism. We discussed recent actions by France against Israel, and I agreed to help organize a boycott against Air France at JFK Airport. It's important that people understand I'm not only for the blacks, but for the Jews, too.

January 17

It was unfortunate that so few people attended services this evening, because I gave one of my best sermons of the season. I pointed out the incongruity between spiritual Israel, to which I link our Jewish heritage and emotion, and the state of Israel, which I fear is turning into a nationalistic, militaristic society. If there is one sure way to turn off a Jewish congregation, it is to attack Israel, even as affectionately as I did. The sermon was prompted by the recent Israeli attack on the Beirut airport.

It was not the first time I had sermonized on Israel. At the end of the Six-Day War in 1967, my congregation in Wheeling arranged a large victory celebration, attended by all the Jews in town. A visiting colonel from the Israeli Army delivered the victory speech. I don't recall his exact words, but I remember his boasting about how many Arabs *we* had killed, how many tanks *we* had captured. The congregation was hysterically responsive. As they cheered on the colonel, they literally bounced with delight in their seats: *I, the shoe salesman, killed an Arab; I, the heart specialist, captured a tank.* I had never seen them so excited, so gloating, so proud of themselves. Then they called on me, as the rabbi, to say a few final words, expecting the appropriate benediction to further celebrate *our* military conquest.

"I only want to say one thing," I said. "I'm pleased that Israel has survived. However, I don't think that an Arab mother weeps for her dead son any differently than a Jewish mother does. I simply refuse to take any joy in the killing of Arab children, any more than I would take joy in the killing of Jewish children."

The congregation was stunned, and the Israeli colonel left without speaking to me.

I favor a Jewish homeland in Israel, I pointed out tonight, a real *homeland:* a cultural center, a religious center, a spiritual center. But instead, I said, I worry that what we have in Israel is a *nation.*

And Israel these days is acting more and more like every other nation, I continued; as time goes on, there is not much particularly Jewish about it. Israelis don't worship Judaism as much as they worship Israel. They seem to have little or no sense of the God of Abraham, Isaac, and Jacob, the God who was above nations, the God of all people. God made a covenant with Noah, a non-Jew, a pre-Jew, before he made a covenant with Abraham, and in my mind that is central to the Jewish experience. It was only when God despaired of this covenant that he made another covenant with Abraham, the Father of the Jews, hoping to use the Jews as an instrument to bring Him in touch once again with all the people. Although in this sense God *chose* the Jews, He never had any intention that they should worship themselves.

The Israelis, I suggested, seem to honor a covenant only with their own nationhood, and, personally, I am opposed to Israeli nationalism as I am to American nationalism.

I explained that I pray for Israel's survival, yet I am distressed by how the Israelis seem to find glory in the way they are surviving. They have come to value that which is required to survive—a large military establishment, which was created out of necessity to meet a threat, but whose very continuation and glorification serves only as an impetus to preserve the threat. How are they going to turn it off?

For these reasons, I told my congregation, I opposed the Israeli attack on the Beirut airport, not for what it was (the

Israelis deliberately destroyed only airplanes, not human lives), but for what it represented. I conceded that, since my first commitment is to the survival of Israel, I may be contradicting myself. But I am not a military tactician. I am a Jew.

After the service, I told someone how much I had enjoyed my sermon. She looked at me as if I were crazy.

Before I left the synagogue, the cantor drew me aside and told me he'd heard that one of the rabbis involved in the McKissick incident was, as he put it, out to get him. He asked me if that were true, and I told him I supposed, in a way, it was. The cantor launched an emotional tirade, filled with empty threats about how he was not without his own resources and how he was going to get the rabbi.

"I am going to ruin that man," he said. "I am going to show him that he is nothing."

Bob Mandel happened to overhear the cantor and warned him that he would be held responsible if he did anything to embarrass the congregation.

There is usually an epilogue to these conversations with the cantor, and tonight's occurred as soon as I reached my home. The phone rang.

"Why don't you tell me more?" the cantor said. "Why don't you tell me all you know?"

"I don't know any more," I said.

"Then you're not my friend," he replied. "It's about time you recognized that we are both nothing more than employees."

January 18

The cantor told me today that the president of the congregation, Bob Mandel, considers me responsible for inciting him against the rabbi involved in the McKissick affair. Of course, this is an attempt on the cantor's part to destroy the relationship between the president and me. He must feel he's going to lose his job, and I guess he'd like some company.

January 20

I went to Washington this morning for the Inauguration, partly to see what it's like at changeover time and to get some clues to the Nixon Presidency, mostly because I thought it would be fun. At the swearing-in, I stood so far back the President was just a dot in the distance. I watched the crowd more than the ceremonies, well-behaved people, proper, moderately well dressed but not stylish, and I noticed that during the prayers offered by Billy Graham and by another Protestant minister, they bowed their heads and closed their eyes. I noticed that during the prayers by a priest and by a rabbi they did not close their eyes.

There were few black people in attendance, and the crowd, although obviously pro-Nixon, was not overly enthusiastic. These were Richard Nixon's Forgotten Americans—small-town people, Southerners, churchgoing people, with neither overt animosity nor overt concern for blacks or Jews. I liked the tone of the President's address: it was low-key, sincere, and reconciliatory.

If he can shift his base and not his tone, I think he will do well.

After the swearing-in, I went to the office of my Congressman, Allard Lowenstein, a Reform Democrat. Lowenstein, in the view of many, is the man most responsible for persuading Eugene McCarthy to challenge Lyndon Johnson in 1968, the man, second only to McCarthy himself, who inspired the new youth movement in American politics. In his Congressional campaign, I served as chairman of Clergymen for Lowenstein and also, since I'm a registered Republican, as a member of Republicans for Lowenstein. As a result, I've had frequent contact with him.

It frustrates me to describe Al Lowenstein, because he is a very elusive man. I suspect that what brought him into politics is not unlike what brought me into the clergy, that peculiar blend of altruism and ego we call a desire to serve, a desire to change the system and a desire to succeed as an individual. Lowenstein has a very formidable ego, a great need to be loved. He constantly surrounds himself with people who adore him. Bright and terribly active, he is not capable of sitting still, has no definite pattern or rhythm of life, and lives rather chaotically, with irregular meals and erratic sleeping habits. This, to me, is immature.

In his own way, Lowenstein is capable of kindness and consideration, and yet he is always distant. When I met him in his office this afternoon, he made a great point of asking me to stay so that he could talk privately to me. Yet he spent so much time mingling with other constituents who were down for the Inauguration, dabbling in little conversations, that we never had our talk. I think he has a certain fear of an intimate, personal encounter. This makes it impossible for me to find out where the man really lives.

But I indict him mostly because I don't think he cares very much about his Congressional district, which includes my community. Even though he is decent, conscientious, and certainly capable—his part in the McCarthy campaign cannot be overestimated—he is too obviously using his role, not serving in it. He has national ambitions.

And then, of course, there's Nixon—with instincts not nearly as hopeful as Lowenstein's—who stands as the champion of community. He is the man who sees the future in terms of small decisions in small communities. That the individual in his own community should direct his own destiny is, essentially, what I have read into Nixon, and this is why he frightens me less than he frightens my friends. I am basically a communalist. Having lived outside New York City for years, I understand that the great work in making this a decent world is a job to be done in communities.

I brought home a souvenir from the Inauguration—a small American flag I bought from an old raggedly dressed lady who could not speak English.

January 21

A couple came to me today to ask me to marry them. He is Jewish and she is Lutheran, and neither of them pretend to have much of a commitment to his own religion and neither of them wants to convert.

I have no preconceived objections to intermarriage—I do object to one of the parties converting to Judaism, unless he or she really wants to convert—but I always ask the same question: Why me? Why not a judge?

Since neither of them had any good answers—apparently, they chose me simply out of convenience—I suggested that they try a different service station.

Later in the day, I had a discussion with a member of my

congregation whose son should be bar mitzvah a year from now. He and his wife are divorced and actively hate one another. He's worried that if the bar mitzvah were to take place, his wife might create a scene during the service to embarrass him. I told him that, if his fears were realistic, there were ways to insure a minimum of disturbance. We could, after all, hire armed guards to protect the temple's doors—which might, if nothing else, be a very symbolic way to bring a boy to manhood in 1970.

I heard today that our building fund is running short, and the congregation is split: some people say that unless we modify our plans and make the building more modest, we can't afford any building at all; others say that if we strip the building any further, it won't be worth putting up. "If we're just going to put up a barn," one member told me, "I'm withdrawing my pledge."

The subcontractor for the building's heating and air-conditioning systems is already calling the proposed synagogue "a castrated building." He happens to be my uncle. He is not a member of our congregation, but he did submit the lowest bid. Really.

I finished the day at a Board of Education meeting at Lawrence High School. Some 800 white parents and students showed up, many of them to complain about beatings and extortions in the school. At one point, a white student, caught up in the spirit of things, rose and asked the board to allow him and his friends to handle the blacks in their own way, assuring everybody that afterward little more would be heard about beatings and extortions at Lawrence. Fortunately, he was ignored.

I wonder if the rabbis of the Talmud had days like this.

January 22

I am trying to decide whether I should build a swimming pool in my garden. If I'm such a greatly concerned person, fighting for justice, then why the luxury of a pool? The question disturbs me. The answer is that I need recreation, just like anyone else, and this is how I want it, I think.

In any case, the decision on the pool has everything to do with my contract renewal. I am inclined to think I would like to remain with the congregation. Breakthroughs are just occurring in the religious school and the style of worship, and we are beginning to feel a sense of community. I don't want to imperil any of this by leaving. On the other hand, I'd like some indication that they would like me to stay. An offer of more money, for instance.

There are rabbis to whom avarice is second nature and who serve their congregations like cautious junior executives. This is not my style. I don't expect my congregants always to agree with me, but I do expect them to respect my freedom to experiment, both in the synagogue and in society.

In this context, the subject of money embarrasses me. I hate the idea of haggling over a few thousand dollars, because I feel I am here for a purpose far above any price tag. I also like to live with the thought that money is not important to me; not important because, even though it is sometimes a consideration, it never detains me from doing what I want to do. Before I became so active in working for the self-destiny of the blacks, I considered the possibility I might lose my job amid the hysteria over the black anti-Semitism. However, the more I thought about it, the sillier I felt thinking about it.

Tonight I feel silly again. I'm about to demand more money for a job I may not have much longer because money is unimportant to me. It's a good thing I don't believe in contradictions. What is *is.*

January 23

The New York *Times,* in a long story starting on its front page today, discovered black anti-Semitism. This puts the stamp of authenticity on the subject. Now the panic among the Jews can turn to terror.

Of course, there *is* black anti-Semitism. Why shouldn't there be? Over the years, as landlords and tradesmen, many Jews have exploited many blacks. But now, in overreacting, in seeing themselves surrounded by tidal waves of black anti-Semitism, some Jews are foolishly appearing to claim all the responsibility for all the white oppression ever perpetrated on blacks.

A few Jewish groups have even gone so far as to organize into militant defense leagues, preparing for an ultimate confrontation, as if the blacks were American Arabs. This, of course, will only create more justification for black anti-Semitism.

The ultimate irony of the situation is that the Anti-Defamation League of B'nai B'rith, originally in the forefront of Jewish organizations helping the causes of the blacks, is now leading the pack in raising the cry of black anti-Semitism. It is curious to me that the ADL should be so vocal at a time when anti-Semitism generally seems to be a fading issue. Could it be that it is difficult to find people willing to donate money to a multi-million dollar organization designed to combat anti-Semitism if there is no anti-Semitism?

This afternoon I attended a meeting in New York of the Clergy Vigil, a group vociferously supporting community control. Although the Vigil is predominantly black, only two black clergymen showed up today. All the others, except me, were white Protestant ministers.

I had come to the meeting with the idea of having the group adopt a statement disavowing anti-Semitism. When I proposed this, the discussion leader, one of the two blacks, threw his hands up and said, matter-of-factly, "We can't do that."

"You can't do that?" I said. "Why?"

"We just can't do that," he said. "That's it." He would give no further explanation.

"But there must be a reason," I insisted.

"If there is any reason," the other black minister said, "it is because you Jews have been taking care of yourselves for a long time, and now we are going to take care of ourselves."

"It's the whole power structure, the whole white establishment, that's been plotting against us," said the discussion leader, "and, very frankly, we don't give a damn about the Jews at this point."

The undertone of this exchange was quite clear. At every conceivable less-than-normal moment for God-knows-how-long, the Jews have cried "anti-Semitism." Nobody cares to listen anymore. I think also these two blacks may have seen me as the rich rabbi from the suburbs, who could not have any understanding, let alone sympathy, for the issue at hand. (I found out later that the discussion leader's mother used to be a maid in the Five Towns.)

"Perhaps I should make one thing clear," I said. "In my opinion, Albert Shanker is not good for the Jews or anybody."

I said I would spend the afternoon demonstrating with them in front of Shanker's office. "And if you want," I said, "I'll tell the press that I feel Shanker created the issue of black anti-Semitism and used it to strengthen his union's position."

They were so startled that the chairman agreed to take up the issue of black anti-Semitism at the next meeting. But he rejected my offer to speak to the press.

"I remember when I was a black token," he said. "They used to drag me in and say, 'Look, we've got a black here and he thinks just like us.' Well we don't want any Jewish tokens, but we do appreciate your goodwill. We believe you are sincere. We understand your position, so you don't have to say anything.

We don't want you to say anything. We want you to be with us."

Later it was decided that four representatives of the Vigil—a priest, a Protestant leader, a black leader and me—would force a personal face-to-face confrontation with Shanker next Monday.

In the afternoon, when I was marching in the picket line with a placard calling for community control, I kept thinking how this issue had made us all actors in a morality play, struggling over which ideology will prevail, struggling to find new relationships among the ideologies—black, white, Jewish—in a time when each ideology somehow feels threatened.

One thing people will surely fight for is their own view of themselves, and the role they have earned in the social order. In their own opinion—and probably rightly so—the Jews have come through a great struggle and have now risen to the top. They don't want to compromise this position, and who, honestly, can blame them? So now they are in a panic, not only over the blacks, but because they fear the nations of the world will impose an unfavorable settlement on Israel. Every unkind word about Israel is viewed by the majority of American Jews as blatant anti-Semitism. They have never learned how to be objective about Israel as a nation—or themselves as Jews.

January 24

My wife celebrated her birthday today at the Woodmere Country Club, and my mother came out from Brooklyn with a number of her friends to join Judith and me. We enjoyed champagne, a birthday cake, and a lovely dinner. My mother and her friends seem to get a great deal of pleasure out of my achievements.

They were impressed by the lavish surroundings of the club, which reassured them that I had "made" it. (An honorary membership in the Woodmere Country Club is one of the fringe benefits of my job; someday, if I can arrange honorary lessons, I may even learn to play golf.)

I felt vindicated today seeing how proud my mother was. When I phoned her from Cornell fifteen years ago to tell her that I'd decided to become a rabbi, she and my father made a special trip to Ithaca to try to talk me out of it. She had two main arguments: first, a rabbi is responsible to too many bosses; second, he doesn't get paid well enough. It was almost like the old punch line: What kind of a job is that for a nice Jewish boy?

Al Lowenstein, my Congressman, called me tonight to suggest that Shirley Chisholm, a black Congresswoman from Brooklyn, speak to my congregation. I liked the idea and checked with Bob Mandel and Al Vorspan, and they both liked it, too. I was pleased by the call from Lowenstein because it showed me that he does have a serious intent, even if it is to be kind of a Super Rabbi to the whole Congressional district.

January 25

After the service this morning, the cantor called me aside. "I just want to tell you one thing," he said. "If I lose my job here, you're coming with me. I promise you that."

I just listened. I don't know what to say to him anymore.

January 26

I went into Manhattan today to perform a wedding. The parents of the bride, the ones who had asked me to officiate, are classic leftists, the sort of people who set aside weekends for picketing. Among the guests at the wedding were women who had chained themselves to the White House fence, men who had planted their bodies beneath the wheels of trucks transporting war materiel, and men and women who had waved placards from Gracie Mansion to the Pentagon. They were truly committed people.

And the wedding was held at the Plaza Hotel, that plush and extravagant castle of capitalism which may be the most expensive place to spend the night—or stage a wedding—in all New York.

I presented a bit of an intellectual crisis to the Plaza liberals. On the one hand, they respect me because I identify with their causes. On the other hand, it is part of their 1930s and 1940s socialistic ideology to see religion as reactionary, a tool of the upper classes to keep the lower classes in bondage.

To them, I am decent, but religion is decadent.

"Rabbi," one sumptuously dressed woman said to me over the hors d'oeuvres, "how much longer do you think you will be able to stay at Temple Sinai? You know, the other day I heard a member of your congregation swear he and his group were going to do everything possible to get rid of you."

Even though I took her remark—and there were others like it—in context, it made me wonder. I'm not naïve. I'd like to believe that there are going to be no serious problems about my contract renewal, but it wouldn't surprise me if those who oppose me are getting prepared for something more than I anticipate.

After the wedding, I stayed for the dinner and had a lot of fun dancing with some of the leftist ladies. They're a pretty *zaftig* group; it must be all that fresh air they get while picketing.

January 27

I am not what you'd call an early riser. I am also not very punctual. I'm generally late for any appointment, and twice as late for a morning appointment.

But this was a special day, and I rose an hour earlier than I had to, checked with my secretary to make certain I had canceled all my other appointments, then rushed into New York. I didn't want to be late for the confrontation between the representatives of the Clergy Vigil and Albert Shanker. I even took the time to draft a statement for the press on the relationship between community control and anti-Semitism.

I showed up on time. No one else did. In fact, no one else showed up at all, not even the man who had planned the confrontation.

I was all alone. I found a few reporters, gave them my statement and went home.

I just don't know what my future relationship with the Clergy Vigil will be. I'm beginning to feel that they're not too anxious to have a rabbi associated with them.

It's really strange. The blacks consider us Jews members of the establishment, but, because of our sense of history, we're incapable of considering ourselves members of any establishment, other than our own. We're as insecure as the blacks—and twice as neurotic.

January 28

Since the fall, I have been teaching a voluntary afternoon class for high-school students at the temple. At the beginning, a dozen students attended more or less regularly, but in recent weeks, fewer and fewer have been showing up. Last week only one student attended.

To avoid a recurrence, the religious-school director phoned each student in the class and asked if he or she planned to come to the next session. They all said they wanted to, but complained the time was not convenient. So we changed the hour and rescheduled the class for this afternoon. Nobody showed up.

I think if I meant something to these students, they would be coming to the class, but I'm afraid I am not reaching them. I tend to think in intellectual, abstract, and universal terms which they're not prepared to deal with. Our only exciting discussion so far has been about whether one should smoke before the age of sixteen. I'm not sure I really understand them, and they sense this. I find it all very frustrating.

Tonight, the board of directors of Temple Sinai voted to go ahead and build our new synagogue—even though the amount of money raised so far is almost $200,000 short of the $700,000 originally budgeted. As of now, there are no provisions for carpeting, painting or lighting in some parts of the building, but the idea is to add these as new fund pledges come in. From what I understand, the heating and air-conditioning systems are definitely going in. My uncle'll be happy to hear that.

The board's decision was unanimous, but it still has to be ratified by a vote of the congregation.

A number of other related resolutions were introduced at the board meeting, touching off some very spirited debate around two issues.

The first was whether members who could afford to but had not contributed to the building fund should be embarrassed out of the congregation. Someone suggested that we publish a list of the people who had contributed. The prevailing feeling at the start of the discussion was that those who do not participate in the community should not be accepted as part of it. It was felt that any person sharing the benefits of the community should be willing to pay the taxes demanded of him, especially if he could afford to. A contribution to the building fund, the argument went, signifies a *real* commitment to the community. Although I agreed with this point of view, I could not reconcile it with the fact that I did not want anybody excluded from a house of worship for any reason. Finally, with reservations, the congregation agreed with me.

The second issue concerned the solicitation of new members. If the congregation fails to grow in the next few years, it will certainly encounter serious financial difficulties. Since we decided to construct a stripped-down building, the general fear of the board was that this might be a deterrent to finding new members. They seemed to feel that Jews, even though they are notoriously apathetic about attending services, are attracted to a congregation by the quality of its building. After more than an hour of involved discussion on the topic, the board voted to impose a surcharge on all new members, presumably to pay for the interior additions to the building they will see mostly from the outside.

January 29

A young man in the confirmation class told me today he doubts whether he wants to be Jewish because he doesn't believe in God.

"I don't believe in God, either," I told him. "But that has nothing to do with being Jewish."

He looked at me rather oddly. "What do you have to believe in?" he asked. "Anything?"

"Judaism is not a system of belief," I said. "Judaism is an effort to try to find some purpose and meaning to your life."

"Yes," he said, "that makes sense. I believe in that."

Living as we do in a Gentile society, I realize that this is not an easy concept for the average student to comprehend. What I tried to do in class this afternoon was explain to the students how Judaism has been distilled from Eastern traditions, and how these traditions differ from their Westernized conditioning.

Western religions, such as Christianity, are essentially theological and rational. Institutions, structures, and forms are their foundation. The orientation is toward the supernatural, and the religions themselves are primarily salvation systems promising eternal life. Christianity, for instance, is, at its core, a kind of Pray Now, Receive Later plan, with the emphasis more on the next life than this one. Christianity is based on absolute truths rather than cumulative wisdom. Western man's morality is one of self-restraint and self-denial leading to eternal reward. In Western religion, God is seen in the form of man.

On the other hand, Eastern religions, such as Judaism and Buddhism, are essentially nontheistic and nonsystematic. The emphasis is on family, community, and people—not institutions, forms, and structures. The orientation is toward *this* world and *this* life; the religious experience is in the moment, in living one's life without self-consciousness. There is no preoccupation with otherworldly salvation. The concern is with wisdom, not truth, and there is nothing which would ever shape God in human form.

In many respects, Judaism has resisted Westernization. Although various attempts have been made to assign it an official theology, all have failed. A Jew must believe only what he wishes to believe, if anything. There have also been numerous efforts to make Judaism rational, but again, none of these has ever been accepted as formative.

The religious reality of Judaism is in its people. Any synagogue is less important than any single Jew. The divine experience is in the community and in the relationships of the people.

In a few areas, Western forces have had a largely unfortunate impact on Judaism. For one, they have encouraged a glorification of the institution, which only serves to cancel out the essence of Judaism. This is why many modern Jews see their synagogue as if it were a church, and end up worshipping the institution while neglecting the substance of their heritage.

Additionally, Jews are having difficulty relating to Judaism because, as members of the Western community, they find themselves having to use Western terms to explain something that is really not Western. For instance, Jews today tend to think of God in the Christian sense, as an omnipotent object, something to believe *in,* something to pray *to,* something to fear. But it's only the Western critical system which demands that God be believed in, not Judaism.

Christian churches proclaim that God is the Creator and that tenets A, B, C, D, and E testify to God's objective omnipotence, and in accepting these, man will qualify to believe in God.

As a result, Westernized Jews find it difficult to realize that *their* God is greater than any explanation, that their God is only a code word, a symbol. Call it the wall, call it the air, call it anything because its only reality is that it stands as a code for that which is real. What is God is that there is more than me in the world, and more than you, and more than me and you, yet, that is what God is—me and you. God is the undiscovered dimension to life which man does not know and will never know, something he can only fleetingly experience through relationships with other humans and, thus, with God. God is the backdrop in front of which man stands.

The powers Western man assigns to God are irrelevant. For instance, it is not important whether God created us. Who cares if he did or he didn't? It's what man himself creates and what man creates with other men and what God creates with us that is real and which stands behind us and in front of us.

A true Jew does not believe *in* God. He believes *that* God can be a vital force in the expression of man's life. People without belief think there is nothing more to them but themselves. How can one look at the great adventure called life, having a genuine feeling for it, if he believes that he himself is so important? In light of what I can be, or what I could do, or in light of how little I really know, how can I be arrogant enough to worship myself? The essence of what I call religion is a realization of the inadequacy of man with respect to all that is around him—a sense of wonder, call it what you will.

Worshipping God has nothing to do with believing *in* Him.

After today's discussion, one confirmation student jumped up and said, "Rabbi, for your information, nobody was listening."

Sometimes, I think Long Island is nothing but sand and *chutzpah.*

Was anybody listening? I tend to be optimistic. Even though a lot of these young people aren't engaging their minds, their minds are being engaged for them, and years from now, when they have forgotten me, I believe they'll remember something I've taught them.

This evening I learned that at least one member of the class was listening. His mother called me and rather bitterly accused me of teaching her child not to believe in God.

January 30

A man needs an occasional retreat from himself. I take mine at the Kiwanis Club where, even if I inhibit the language, I get my back slapped and people call me "Marty." Since religion is an experience completely outside the life of an average Kiwanian, I am able to avoid the shop talk while taking the opportunity to unwind and discover, rather pleasantly, how unimportant I am.

January 31

I'm working simultaneously on a number of writing projects, including this diary, a column for a Catholic newspaper, an article for the national Reform Jewish magazine on the future of the synagogue, and an anthology on Jewish-Christian thought. My most important project, however, is a book on a phenomenon we may be about to witness which I call the Judaization of Christianity.

My publisher for this book is Herder and Herder. The editor they've assigned to the project is a man I've never met who lives in Chicago. About a month ago, he wrote me a brutal letter in which he said he felt that the book had little value. He indicated I had some "fine" thoughts, but he didn't like my style at all and he liked the way I developed my thesis even less.

Even though some of the criticisms were valid, I think he was nothing short of nasty in the way he phrased them. The letter really affected me, and since receiving it, I have not done any further work on the book. In a way, I've been feeling sorry for myself, but also I've had little incentive to keep working with a person who has more regard for style than substance.

A week ago, I got a letter from a Herder editor in New York. His feeling was that my work presented a valid theological alternative and he said he hoped that I would continue to work on it. He said that the changes needed were not so momentous as they seemed and he would like to work with me on making them. This morning I got back to work on the book, making changes and rather enjoying it.

Most of all, I want the book published. But since I feel that this diary has a far greater chance of commercial success and also opens up the possibility of me becoming an ephemeral public personality, I'll wait until it is published before I push my other work. If this approach succeeds, I might even end up talking about the Judaization of Christianity on Johnny Carson's show. I'd like to be in my Chicago editor's bedroom that night.

The old building is now being torn down, and until the new one is up, we will be holding our regular services at a temporary location in the Masonic Temple. In the process of changing over, I got some idea of what Ringling Brothers must go through every time they hit a new location.

At four o'clock this afternoon, a rehearsal was scheduled for the ladies of the Sisterhood, who were to participate in part of the service. When the ladies and I arrived, the folding chairs were not yet set up and nobody knew where anything was. Not until two hours later, when Bob Mandel arrived from his office in New York, were we able to find some of the things we needed. We used up another hour hunting for the key to the organ. Then we found we needed two screens to block off the altar, and we dispatched somebody after them. A few moments later, we realized we still needed flowers, and somebody else was sent to find a florist who was still open.

All of this clearly shows the unfortunate extent to which stage management is a part of religion, because if we hadn't gotten things in order by the start of the service—which miraculously we did—we would have had some real difficulty with some of the stalwarts in the congregation. As it was, there was only my sermon to displease them. I spoke about the community's reaction to the hanging of nine alleged Jewish spies in Iraq this week. I cited that, despite our hysteria, the problem was not so much that Jews had been murdered, but that men had been murdered. On hearing the topic, they had expected the usual denunciation of Iraq and the usual plea for saving the Jews.

February 1

Normally, the difficulties in arranging the service last night would have upset the cantor, but this morning, for some unaccountable reason, he was cheerful, friendly, and warm. He even offered to work with me on a number of projects. Maybe this is the beginning of a new cycle.

This evening I met an older couple whose daughter had married a black man and was now pregnant with his child. They were much too exuberant about it—repeating again and again how they identified with blacks and how they have always been committed to one liberal cause after another. The message was clear: *Look at us. We're going to have a black grandchild, the ultimate in black-white understanding.* I think they were really very upset about the whole thing.

It made me wonder how I would feel about having a black grandchild. Since my main concern is that Judaism be carried on by my daughter, I don't think I'd have any objection if she married a Jewish black man. Jews have been associated with black people in the past. In Biblical times, Jews married blacks, so there is probably some black blood in every Jew, and, come to think of it, some Jewish blood in every black.

The joke is on you, Albert Shanker.

February 2

This evening, before the lecture by Shirley Chisholm, the black Congresswoman from Brooklyn, Congressman Al Lowenstein held a reception at his home in Long Beach. Lowenstein had been hit by a truck in Washington earlier in the week; his arm was in a sling and he was obviously in pain, but he still hosted the reception. Because I find Al very complex, I'm always looking for clues to his character when I'm around him. I noticed tonight that he *appears* to have many intimate friends. He kisses people, particularly the older women, and spends much time with the young people who surround him and seem drawn to him. I have never seen him without four or five very bright young people in his entourage. The look in their eyes is something I can only call love. They worship this man. He also seems very close to them—in fact, he *seems* close to everybody—but I'm not really sure he is close to anybody. Perhaps this is a small key to him: he needs people to be close to him, even intimate, but always in a way that is not personal. He seems to prefer acolytes to associates.

When we left his house, I offered to give Lowenstein a ride. I wanted the unusual opportunity to be alone with him for half an hour. In the car, just the two of us, I sensed he felt a bit uncomfortable without his acolytes.

"What are you doing next week?" I asked him.

"Oh," he said, "I'm going to Africa." He said it as if he were going to Manhattan.

"I guess you're going to settle the Nigerian civil war," I said.

"Yes," he answered. He was dead earnest.

A most unusual fellow.

More than 500 people attended Mrs. Chisholm's lecture. She is a deeply warm and human person and in the few times I've talked to her, I've felt an extraordinary communication. She is genuinely selfless, one of a nearly extinct breed whose motives are beyond question. What she *says,* she *means.* Several months ago she had a serious operation and this was quite evidently on her mind as she spoke to the young people in the audience. "I'm not going to be here for very long," she said, "and you are the people who have to carry on. You are the people who have got to show the way to black-white cooperation in one society."

She pleaded with us to understand that the blacks did have justifiable grievances, just as the Jews did. "The Jews," she said, "have been our friends throughout time, and we, as blacks, should not let ourselves be turned off by a few recent incidents which may not look so good. We've always known that in the clutch we could depend on the Jews."

I think the evening moved many people. It was most inspiring watching all those people willing to listen to a black woman.

As we were leaving the temple, one of the black ladies who had accompanied Mrs. Chisholm from Bedford-Stuyvesant, the Brooklyn ghetto, discovered that her car had a flat tire. I suggested that she leave the car on the street, and in the morning I would call a garage, have the tire repaired, and send the car back to her.

"I could never do that," she said. "If I leave the car here all night, somebody will strip it."

That indicates the kind of brutal existence in which these people must survive.

February 3

I slept late and spent the little that was left of the morning working on revisions for the Herder book. In the afternoon, I participated in a demonstration against Iraqi brutality and against something else, although I forget precisely what, that has to do with the Arabs.

Tonight a small subcommittee of the Five Towns Coalition, a local do-good group, met to plan a few projects. There are nearly 3,500 domestics living in our community and another 5,000 who commute daily to their jobs here, very few of whom enjoy either sick-leave benefits or Social Security. I proposed tonight that the coalition work out a code of ethical personnel practices for those domestics. Only four women were present at the meeting and the one I would have characterized as the most outspokenly liberal resisted my proposal. Maybe I struck too close to home.

February 5

In my Woodmere Academy class, we got into a discussion of loyalty to a universal God. The students asked to what extent Judaism limited them and to what extent they could be universal through Judaism. I told them that as Jews they were not expected to believe in anything in particular precisely because the emphasis was on a universal community. I said that universalism does not mean that people find the sameness of views, but that people, through their own individuality, are able to reach a level of communication which allows for their differences. This is why the structure of Judaism virtually allows each synagogue to be an autonomous community, as opposed to, say, the rigid hierarchy in Catholicism, where moral rules are dictated downward from the Pope.

In the evening, I went to a meeting of our committee on worship. They were still talking about the boy who neglected to wear a coat and tie to the Youth Service three weeks ago.

February 6

I am still agonizing about my swimming pool, but it's not because of my social conscience. To me, a pool is only a pool. It's not a symbol. It's not an indication of stature, of the fact that I've reached a certain level of success. I don't see any particular value in affluence. But on the other hand, there's certainly no virtue in poverty.

That's how I feel about my swimming pool. While there may be no virtue in building it, there is none in not building it, either.

But there are certain practical problems. Judith, for instance, is not certain she wants a pool. I feel we can afford it, but she is very conservative about money. She has been brought up in the tradition of not spending money unnecessarily. Her father is a wealthy man, but he still shops for his groceries at a commissary on a naval base near his South Carolina home. Judith herself is very self-denying, spending virtually nothing on clothes and other personal items.

On the other hand, I enjoy spending money. I make it and I like to spend it. Judith and I have had so many disagreements over the pool that, recently, I just stopped talking about it. I brought up the subject again yesterday. "If you want it," she said, "go ahead and build it." She wasn't exactly enthusiastic.

Another consideration is that, while the pool itself will cost me $7,000, the land on which I plan to build it, a lot adjoining my home, is worth at least $20,000 unimproved. If I ever needed money desperately, I could sell off the lot; the empty lot gives me some flexibility.

I never want to be in the position where I'm locked into this community, where, no matter the conditions, I can't afford to get out. Thus, the issue of the swimming pool is giving me first-hand experience on the confinements of affluence. If indulgence surrenders freedom, self-denial safeguards it. I want the freedom not to stay at this job if I don't care to stay at it and the courage not to force the issue if they don't want me. For the meantime, that means no swimming pool.

I've decided to let the congregation open up the negotiations about my contract. They know there are many other opportunities available to me. They should also know that they are going to have to pay me more, give me better working conditions, a longer vacation, and a lengthier contract. If they really want me, and I hope right now that they do, waiting for them to open up the discussion on the contract will put me in a stronger position. As time goes by, they'll have a diminishing chance to get another rabbi. Certainly, if they wanted to, they could replace me, but with a temporary building and a temporary rabbi, they'd be in trouble.

I hope they bring up the contract soon. I'd like to have my swimming pool in time for summer.

February 7

I slept late this morning because I was up half the night with my two-year-old daughter, Sally. Usually when she wakes up crying, I don't hear her, but last night I did. Judith's strategy is to let her cry. Mine isn't. I picked her up and brought her into bed with us, and it was daylight by the time she let me get back to sleep.

Early in the afternoon I arranged for the farewell service for the old synagogue to be held next Friday evening. Then I called our rabbi emeritus, Rabbi Goodman, to invite him to conduct the service.

"You can't extinguish the eternal light on Friday," he told me, rather sternly.

I guess it has something to do with the Sabbath, but since I regard the issue as unimportant, I agreed to shift the service to Sunday. I suppose I'll now be accused of being weak and vacillating, but I saw no point in making an issue out of something I didn't care about. I believe in compromising where I can, because there are enough legitimate areas in which I don't care to compromise.

Tonight I gave another one of my better sermons: Can Modern Man Worship? I said that the social noise has made it difficult for modern man to hear what people are saying, and communication today tends to aid confusion instead of understanding. Man has taught himself to be an expert talker, I said, but he is forgetting how to listen. Prayer is essentially high-powered communication, and modern man seems to have a diminishing ability to communicate.

I had the unusual feeling that I was getting through to the congregation. Their unconscious reactions give them away, the degree to which they fidget, or yawn, or try not to yawn. Tonight they were especially alert. Afterward several women told me they thought the sermon was *beautiful.*

I don't think a sermon should be judged on the basis of whether or not it is *beautiful,* or successful, or whether people like it. It should be judged solely on whether I have anything to say, which I usually, although not always, do. A sermon is a forty-times-a-year production and there are not many people I know who can wax inspirational, spiritual and/or truthful forty times a year. I am usually at my best when, like tonight, only a small group attends the service, which is ironic: I would like to have more people hear me when I'm this good.

After the service, I attended a dialogue sponsored by the Long Island Congress of Racial Equality (CORE) at the home of one of the left-wing members of my congregation. A number of styles were represented. First, the older, strictly doctrinaire leftists. Second, the white radicals, the let's-go-picket-the-teachers-union types who find status in getting arrested, a relatively immature element who must prove to themselves that they belong, and the only way they can belong is to become human obstacles to social equanimity. Third were the African pseudo-culturists done up in Afro hairdos, dashikis, hats, and primitive jewelry. They also represent a form of immaturity by trying to find some authentic role to play while obviously all wound up in a complex love-hate relationship—wanting and hating what they want.

There seems to be a pattern for meetings like tonight's which pair black militants with whites. First of all, the blacks are always late. They then arrive angry and use their anger as a standard invocation. Once they get this out—by telling us how they feel, by showing us how enraged they are by all that has happened to them—they feel a little better. They relax and they are not quite as angry. When the whites are Jews, like tonight, there is a standard comeback: *we have suffered, too.* This doesn't seem to interest the blacks. Also standard.

In the course of tonight's dialogue, the old leftists, as could be expected, turned the conversation to the *tactics* of the Black Revolution. The mother of the Plaza wedding made some point about our whole society being corrupt and decadent, which pretty much set the tone. Everybody seemed to feel that if the blacks were to denounce violence, they would be limiting their options. I seemed to be the only one advocating nonviolence.

They asked me what I thought nonviolence was. I told them nonviolence simply means that we don't destroy—or destroy as little as possible—in the process of creating. When they pressed further, I told them I felt that the real issue was not violence or nonviolence, but maturity or immaturity.

If an adolescent is angry at society and shows his frustration by driving a car fast, he runs the risk of getting killed. Perhaps there is nothing society can do to make the youth drive slower, but it certainly doesn't have to condone him. By the same token, there is no reason for mature whites to glorify immature actions of the blacks, such as their habit of showing up late to meetings like this. "There are better ways to make your point if you have to," I told the militants tonight.

The blacks, as a people, are in their adolescent period. Deep down, I suspect, they are afraid to deal with whites as equals. The mothers of the militants still work as maids. Their talk of violence is just an expression of fear, and the more they talk violence, the more backlash they breed and the further they remove themselves from what they rightly deserve. They just can't go around threatening violence. Whites are not going to give in under the threat of violence because it would mean inviting their own destruction.

The most inspiring thing about tonight's session was that I heard the blacks through their words. They came brimming for confrontation, but with some encouragement, they proved adept at dialogue. I learned a lot. I learned to see the Black Revolution as a movement toward selfhood. I believe that CORE is an authentic black group. I asked them if I could join. They said they accept very few whites, and I noticed that the only white CORE member present tonight strongly supported looting and burning.

But they later said they might accept me in CORE.

February 8

A dozen members of my congregation gathered this afternoon for the *Havdalah* service, the service ending the Sabbath, and, afterward, for a discussion of the meaning of Jewish identity. Each person in his own way came to the conclusion that there was something different, something unique, something special about being Jewish. They may have used euphemisms, but their general feelings were clear: to be Jewish is to be superior.

These people, like most modern Jews, obviously regard themselves as a "chosen" people, a view which distresses me, not because it's untrue, but because their reasoning is faulty. To them, the something special about being Jewish is that more Jews have won more Nobel Prizes and more Jews have gained more Ph.D's and more Jews have earned more money; they count numbers, not commitment, and they label people Jewish by birth, not by conviction. To me, the something special—and there is something very special—about being a Jew is the humanism of Judaism, of the religion.

Jewish people are heir to the most civilized heritage in the Western world, a heritage which has had and will continue to have a great effect on humanizing our relatively immature Christian civilization. We are in fact, according to my own theory, just entering a period of Jewish-Christian reconciliation in which the world will ultimately adhere to a form of Judaism and call it Christianity, a world in which individuals will share a humane—not a programmed—public responsibility, a world as concerned for men as for mankind, a world which will encourage personal involvement in the humanity of the individual experience.

All this may sound superior, and to a large extent it is. But it is a special destiny we as Jews have. We have been accused as a people of being arrogant, but the only arrogant Jews are those who don't live up to Judaism. Which means most modern Jews.

February 9

Fifteen inches of snow fell today, and my phone rang all morning, mostly people calling to find out whether the religious school was still on. It was canceled, and so was a congregational meeting to ratify the board's decision on the new building.

One of my callers this morning told me that he had heard some people complaining to our president, Bob Mandel, that I was responsible for the McKissick affair. The fact that the incident is now two months old and people haven't forgotten it shows the depth of fear and frustration in this community. The man who called me said that there was a definite effort on the part of some people to get me known as the radical rabbi in order to force the congregation to fire me.

February 10

The snow reached to three and four feet in drifts in front of my house. Everything scheduled for the day was canceled.

Sally and I went walking in the snow, and I was amazed at how warm and friendly everybody was. It wasn't like this community at all. When I moved here from Wheeling, I was in the habit of saying hello to people in the streets, but after too many fishy-eyed looks, I gave it up.

Once the snow melts, I imagine the people will freeze up again.

February 11

We're still virtually stranded, and Judith and I spent part of the day working out our finances. We have the classic marital setup. She is in charge. I turn over my check to her each month and she pays the bills and gives me pocket money as I need it. My domain is our investments, and since we have a substantial portfolio of stocks and bonds, I delight every now and then, like today, in sitting down and figuring out how much I am worth.

February 12

I went to dig out my car this morning, and as I bent over to start shoveling—CRACK—I fell over in terrible pain.

Some neighbors who had been watching me from their windows rushed out and carried me into the house. The doctor came and gave me a pain-killer and told me to spend the day lying on my back. My only form of mobilization was crawling.

February 13

I was able to walk around a little today, and while I stopped taking the drug for pain, I continued to take one to relax my muscles. This morning a gentleman called to make an appointment to see me, and he arrived punctually at 2 P.M., quite decently dressed. He was the first schnorrer to visit me this year. A schnorrer is a beggar, and schnorring is an honored Jewish profession.

I am an easy mark for schnorrers because I believe that if an individual is going to degrade himself to the point of asking for money, the least I can do is give it to him. The gentleman said he needed money for a snow tire and dinner.

Because his visit was somewhat out of season, it surprised me. Most schnorrers work this area only in the spring and fall, then spend their winters in Miami and their summers in the Catskill Borscht Belt in New York State. Wherever they travel on this circuit, their first target is often the local rabbi. I gave the gentleman a check for $15, and he quite ceremoniously accepted it, borrowed my phone to call ahead to the rabbi in the next town, and left.

To take care of these things, I administer a small private trust of a few thousand dollars, most of it donated by people for me to spend at my discretion. In Wheeling, one man would donate at least a thousand dollars a year. I use the money for a variety of purposes, not the least of which is to finance schnorrers. I have also helped students through college and, where a small amount of money is the basis of a problem for which people come to see me, I help them, too. One of the more unusual things I've done recently was to send a young man suffering from an identity crisis to Mexico with two girl friends. The young man had been previously involved with drugs, and a wealthy man, who knew him and who wanted to "save" him in the Christian sense, donated $1,800 to my tax-exempt trust, asking that I pass it on to the threesome so the young man could spend a few months finding himself in Mexico.

February 14

The pain in my back has diminished to a numb, steady discomfort, and I was well enough to conduct services this evening. Since more of my congregation shows up on Friday night than on Saturday, one of my innovations has been to read from the Torah every fifth Friday. The Torah contains the deepest level of Jewish experience, and tonight's portion dealt with the Jewish laws for slavery, which when studied are further testimony to the humanity of Jewish civilization. Four thousand years ago, Jewish law prescribed that slaves (who were also Jews) be treated as human beings with rights, not as property, and that the period of enslavement be limited, a form of slavery certainly less barbaric than the American version one hundred years ago.

After the service, I converted a young man who was Protestant to Judaism. He is planning to marry a Jewish girl, and for several months I have been giving him lessons. Despite his open mind and open heart, he has not been a particularly good student, yet—more importantly—he has shown himself to be serious and conscientious about converting. He talks enthusiastically about the warmth and friendliness of the Jewish people, and wants very much to belong to our community. I believe a man should choose his religious experience, not by his beliefs, but by the community in which he cares to participate, and for this reason this young man's conversion represents a small triumph for the Jewish heritage.

Like this young man, most non-Jews who convert to Judaism do so because they are about to marry a Jew. Unlike this case, the conversion too often is a pointless exercise to placate the rankled Jewish parents, to make possible a Jewish wedding, and to create the illusion that the couple intends to carry on a Jewish existence together. Since most rabbis won't perform interfaith weddings, the conversion is a prerequisite to enlisting the rabbi and renting the synagogue.

Since I believe that Judaism is a very special heritage, I don't like giving it away simply as a matter of convenience. As a rabbi I feel obligated to stand guard for the future of Jewish peoplehood, and I'd rather have a dozen genuine Jews than a million diluted ones.

Always at the forefront of my mind is that my role in my little moment of life is to represent the continuation of the Jewish experience. When two people who wish to marry come to see me and one wants to convert (because this is New York, often they will pick my name from the Yellow Pages), the first thing I ask myself is that if I perform this conversion and wedding, what will I be saving for Judaism? I usually hold an interview or two in which I do everything I can to discourage the non-Jewish partner from converting. I warn that Jews suffer terrible discrimination, that Jews are narrow-minded, that a Jewish identity can be a lifetime liability in many situations. Sometimes—not often—I do discourage them, or at least they don't come back to me. But who knows? They probably just go back to the Yellow Pages.

If I fail to discourage them, and I sense that, despite their different backgrounds, they are probably suited for marriage, I usually offer to conduct the ceremony as an agent of the state, with all religious references deleted, and no conversion necessary. If they continue to challenge me, I ask them why they want a rabbi to marry them, and it is in their answer to this that I usually make my final decision. I do not look for an intellectually sound response; I look for something that indicates a genuine commitment to Judaism, like the young man I converted this evening who had told me he felt he wanted to belong to our community.

It's not a question of my team versus their team. I just don't like to give Judaism away easily. I am not opposed to Christianity. To the contrary, I find great value in it. It allows us Jews to be special.

I also am not against Christians converting to marry Jews. However, the fact is that Jews are raised differently than Christians, and even though the differences may be subtle, they can often be the basis for later conflict. Christians are a product of their Western intellectual heritage and, as such, are inclined to see things in terms of moral principles, Right and Wrong, Good and Bad. In Judaism, morality is a tradition to be carried on through the vehicle of the family, rooted not in these absolutes, but in charity, mercy, and humanity. Consciously or not, every Jew is to some degree a product of this heritage, if for no other reason than that was the way his mother raised him.

Because—obviously—there are many modern Jews who hardly exemplify Judaism, and there are many Christians who in effect live Jewish lives, the incongruity of backgrounds does not always preclude a successful interfaith marriage. Each couple has to be dealt with individually. But my inclination is always to give the benefit of the doubt to the future of Judaism. If I feel a couple regards conversion as just another checkmark on the list of things to do before the marriage ceremony, I turn them down. At this moment in its existence, the last thing Judaism needs is more marginal Jews.

February 15

The cantor got stuck behind a broken-down truck and couldn't get to services this morning, so I had to do double duty: reading and singing the service. If my congregation is willing to put up with my singing, there is hope for any kind of experimentation in our services.

February 16

The Synagogue Council of America, one of those umbrella organizations in the Jewish establishment, has asked me to serve on a special committee it has established to study the community-control issue. Jews have always regarded themselves as progressive people, and now this issue, with its imagined undertone of black anti-Semitism, is forcing an intensive self-reexamination. However, I don't feel that the reexamination will do any good unless the Jews first come to terms with two basic realities.

First is their fixation on anti-Semitism. Every individual Jew has a tendency to think of himself as all Jews. If he suffers personal discrimination he calls it anti-Semitism.

Even when it does exist, anti-Semitism is in the nature of things. Jews are different—they recognize this and they thrive on it—and as long as they are going to be different, they should be prepared for the fact that they are going to encounter prejudice. As it is, their neuroticism about anti-Semitism prevents Jews from understanding that there may indeed be people who do have valid grievances against them.

Second is the reality that the Jewish establishment is so self-involved and so terribly busy with its own internal politics that it finds itself unable to make the basic changes required to deal with the new situation. At this point, the most constructive thing some of the establishment organizations could do would be to eliminate themselves.

Unfortunately, the organizations are consumed with one purpose: perpetuating themselves. While they feud over which one will be the official spokesman for *all* Jews in the New York *Times* (where they measure their influence in column inches), they remain oblivious to the reality that their base is disappearing from beneath them. They have lost touch, particularly with the young, and they are no more the authentic leaders of the Jews than Whitney Young and Roy Wilkins are authentic black leaders.

Tonight the congregation met to ratify the board's decision to put up the new building, a matter most of us felt would be a formality. Then one man rose and said he represented a group which was unhappy with the possibility of starting a project we had no funds to complete adequately. "We don't want an ugly building," he said.

He and his "group" felt that the congregation should wait until it had the necessary finances to put up an adequate building. "To be quite frank," he later admitted, "the building is not very important to me. My children are grown and I won't have very much use for it."

At this, a woman in her early seventies jumped up. "Well, I have no children," she said angrily, "and I don't even know whether I'll live to see the building completed, but I'm going to do everything I can to see it go up, so that we all can go on living as a Jewish people."

She was applauded.

This seemed to be the turning point. With only one couple against it (I understand they vote against *everything*), the building project was approved.

As the meeting ended, five or six people, quietly and without public notice, increased their contributions for the skylight fund. It looks like, if nothing else, we definitely are going to have a skylight—for more direct communication upstairs, I suppose.

By the time the building is completed and furnished, it will probably cost upward of $1,250,000, and yet it will be nowhere near as lavish as the four-star synagogue in this community.

February 17

This is Brotherhood Week or Brotherhood Month, I always forget which. It's all so pointless. As usual, however, Brotherhood Week-or-Month was the occasion for an interfaith luncheon to which I and a half dozen other clergymen were invited. We were asked to discuss the changing role of women in society. After the Catholic priest gave his idealized view of women, I got up and spoke about the disintegration of family life. Not sticking to the assigned subject was my own quiet rebellion against formalized, lip-service brotherhood.

February 18

I spoke to the Hadassah group in Laurelton, Long Island, this morning. It's customary for a group such as this to give the speaker a small fee, and though it's nothing substantial, I usually look forward to it. Today the president of the chapter told me as I was leaving that the group would make a donation to the Hadassah Medical Center in my honor. *Their* charity—*my* money.

The chairman of the worship committee suggested tonight that we give a plaque to the cantor in recognition of his seventeen years of service to the temple. Because I think he deserves it, I was in favor of the proposal, but the majority of the committee voted it down. There were numerous complaints about him: too argumentative, too emotional, too lazy. Somebody railed against him because he crosses his legs on the pulpit, and a few people protested that he always has a distracted, bored look on his face during services. There is some suspicion, perhaps justified, that, if the cantor could have a phone on the pulpit, he'd carry on his lecture business without missing a note. The discussion grew so heated that I feared, instead of giving him a plaque, they would pass a resolution to fire him on the spot.

February 20

I went to New York City today to see my stockbroker and to attend a meeting at the Synagogue Council of America.

The SCA, which is involved in an intramural civil war with some of the other Jewish establishment groups, accomplished a minor coup recently when it received a Ford Foundation grant to develop a dialogue between blacks and whites. The purpose of today's meeting was to figure out how to spend the money. It turned out to be one of those gatherings at which everybody gets up and gives his discourse whether or not it is related to anything else. After an hour or so of sermons, I gave up and went home.

February 21

This evening, toward the end of a Five Towns Coalition committee meeting, Mrs. Allard Lowenstein became ill and had to be driven home. With Al running all over as he does, it must be very difficult for her. He just returned from ten days in Africa and is off somewhere again. Meanwhile, she is pregnant and living in a new community, with a small child and few friends.

February 22

I learned today that a seventy-year-old man who worked one day a week for $15.80 as the custodian of our synagogue has been fired as an economy move. After services this morning, I took Bob Mandel aside and asked him to reinstate the custodian.

"Are you asking me on the basis of charity, mercy or justice?" he asked.

"Charity," I said.

"Well, on that basis, we'll reinstate him."

I usually don't do that well with multiple-choice questions.

February 23

The farewell service for the old building was conducted this afternoon by me and our rabbi emeritus, Rabbi Goodman. The service was filled with nostalgic speeches by Bob Mandel, Rabbi Goodman, and a rabbi from another synagogue which had once used our building as temporary quarters. In my speech, I urged the congregation to seek relevant Judaism outside the world of catering halls.

At the end of the service, the eternal light was extinguished and we prepared to move the Torahs to a new, temporary home. I was supposed to carry out one Torah, but because of my back, I couldn't. The cantor was also supposed to carry a Torah, but through an error, he was not listed in the program as one of the Torah carriers. As Bob Mandel and the worship committee chairman were lifting their Torahs, the cantor started to walk away.

"I'm not carrying a Torah," he said.

"What?" said Bob Mandel, startled.

"Give it to the rabbi," the cantor said, loud enough to be heard by some members of the congregation. "Let him carry it."

"He can't carry it because of his back," the president answered.

The cantor then turned around, grabbed the Torah, and stormed out. "I'm the nigger of this congregation," he muttered. "I don't get any rights, and nobody listens to me. Why should I do this? Why should I carry the Torah? It's hypocrisy for me to be doing this."

February 24

Judith and I and my mother left this morning for a four-day vacation at a place called the Harbor Island Spa in New Jersey. It's what I call a nonsectarian Jewish retreat; there are no cultural or religious programs of any kind, but every single guest is a Jew. An overweight Jew, to be exact.

There are none of the traditional Jewish resort trappings, such as kosher food and mink coats. They serve anything you want to eat, but the food is dietetic, which means we all go virtually hungry. The major attractions are the health facilities—saunas, steam rooms, sunken whirlpool baths, and a pool. Guests are entitled to one free massage per day, and our activities revolve around it.

When I first arrived, I was determined to remain unofficial. I went to make an appointment for my first daily massage and the man asked me my name.

"Martin Siegel," I said.

He was rather rough, and not particularly polite. In fact, he was nasty.

Later on, he found out somehow that the man he had registered was in fact *Rabbi* Martin Siegel.

"Why didn't you tell me you were a rabbi?" he asked.

"I didn't think it was necessary," I said.

"Well, it's a pleasure to have you here, Rabbi, and let us know if we can do anything to make your stay more comfortable."

Now they even treat me piously in the sauna bath.

February 25

Everybody seems pleased to have a rabbi around. They got a kick out of passing me the ham at the dinner table.

All day long, we played Jewish geography. "Do you know my rabbi in Brooklyn?" they asked. "Do you know my rabbi in Great Neck?"

I saw a newspaper this afternoon and noticed that members of my group, the Clergy Vigil, were arrested yesterday for trespassing on Board of Education property while demonstrating for community control. I'd probably be in jail right now —if I hadn't come to the Harbor Island Spa.

February 26

We left today, a day early, because I got tired of resting.

February 27

I attended a meeting this morning of the Religious Council of the Five Towns, a local interfaith clergy group I serve as corresponding secretary, which means my office staff sends out the meeting notices. Communication within the group is very poor. The one Catholic priest who attends acts like a special delegate from the Vatican. The ministers are, for the most part, frustrated by their dwindling congregations, and there is a slight undertone of resentment against the rabbis in the group, probably because of the Jewish predominance in this area.

In today's discussion, we got into the black-white confrontation. Most of the rabbis were obviously antagonistic toward the blacks. One came right out and said he would never let a black man step into his synagogue. He could turn me anti-Semitic. As a matter of fact, he probably thinks I already am.

This evening I met with a small group interested in broadening Temple Sinai's activities. In discussing the present temple membership, the group agreed that only a core of about thirty percent of the members have a genuine interest in the temple, in each other and in Judaism. Fifty percent, they said, have a general peripheral interest, fifteen percent a special interest (the Men's Club, the bowling league or the Sisterhood) and five percent have an ephemeral interest. Members of this last group join until the services they require (bar mitzvahs, confirmations, weddings) are completed, then quit.

All this only reaffirms my theory that the synagogue is near its death. In fact, if its vitality is to be measured by the impact it has on the lives of its members, it is already dead. This process began several decades ago. Hitler only interrupted it. When the slaughter was all over, American Jews began to see that they, too, could have been in those ovens, a realization which led temporarily to a Jewish religious revival.

But, underneath, the decline continued unabated until today, twenty-five years later, the glory of a synagogue is measured by the size of its membership and the grandeur of its ballroom. The genuine religious impulse on which the synagogue was founded has been so perverted it has rendered the institution spiritually lifeless—and possibly dangerous.

Simultaneous to these developments something I call the A-B-C progression has been going on. Generation A, the grandparents and the great-grandparents of today's youth, believed in the old God of might and power, the God who could cure them, the God who could save them, and the God who could give them more than life. Although medieval in their pattern of beliefs, these people lived with overwhelming deference to something greater than themselves, and with a humility for their own existence. Generation B, their children, were humanists, pragmatists, and materialists who found their own life-styles ill-suited to this view of God. Yet the experience of simply knowing people like their parents, whose lives were so moved by God, prevented them from giving up the beliefs. As a result, they accepted the forms of God-worship without ever truly relating to the substance of it. Judaism didn't really ever mean anything to them—in their secular pursuits, they failed to understand it —but it had meant so much to their parents that they could not allow themselves to become the last generation of Jews. Instead, they became mechanical Jews, carrying on the forms, but not moved by the religious impulse. Generation C, their children and today's youth, are the inheritors of this brand of Judaism.

The pity of this metamorphosis is that the kids today, legitimately turned off by the synagogue as an anachronism where people worship empty forms in the name of Judaism, are rejecting Judaism itself when they don't even know what it really is. Therefore, probably only in replacing the institution will the substance of Judaism be preserved. For these reasons, I don't lament the passing of the synagogue.

I believe the synagogue must be fossilized to make way for

a new expression of man's religious impulse. In the interim, we will probably be turning to the new secular religion of pop festivals, sex or drugs, but ultimately, given free reign, man will again create worthy new institutions to give expression to his timeless need for meaning, his timeless yearning to stay in touch with the cosmos. The synagogue is plainly an expression of another era, as out of place as a romantic painting in a gallery of pop art.

Without a synagogue, I, as a rabbi, will be out of business, but because I feel the Jewish people will survive the demise of their institutions, this is something I welcome. It has always been my fantasy that someday I could work at something else—whether it be teaching or selling vacuum cleaners—while serving as a rabbi in my spare time for those genuinely concerned with discovering the religious dimension to their existence. I'm amazed at how attractive I find the communes, the experimental communities, because I think they are the places where men in the future will find meaning to their lives.

February 28

I got wound up in my sermon tonight and used the term "empty-headed Jewish pagans" to describe those modern Jews whose only values are those created by other men. Our traditional Jewish educational system has a way of producing pagans because its primary concern is with doling out information, not with helping in the important development of attitudes and understanding. As a result, too many Jews are going through life without ever connecting the values of Judaism to the quality of their existence.

After the service the father of a young man who will be bar mitzvah shortly asked to speak to me privately.

"My son," he said, "is quite upset that you called him an empty-headed Jewish pagan."

March 1

Our monthly Sabbath afternoon discussion group today tackled the question: What does it mean to have religion? One man, an editor and a trained physicist, said religion relates us to the cosmos—the more we learn about physical things the more we realize we don't know, the greater our sense of wonder. In his view, religion can relate us to the ultimates in life, even if we don't care to accept its philosophical qualities. Another fellow, a speech professor, felt that religion is a way of dealing with and relating to people.

A former Catholic priest sat in on the discussion, and his contribution was quite interesting. He said that the purpose of religion was to relate us to our Maker. If you're here, he reasoned, then you have to have a Maker. (Ironically, it is this sort of thinking which is contributing to the collapse of the Catholic Church.)

I rejected the priest's view. I talked about the late Martin Buber who wrote and taught that reality is in the relationship. In what he called the I-Thou expression, reality can't be objective, because it's only relational. That is, there is you and there is me, and we have a relationship, in which I am an object and you are an object. We can see, feel, hear, smell, and touch each other but only when the whole of me is communicating with the whole of you are we both changed by the experience, or do we have an I-Thou relationship. God is in this relationship, in the small moments between us which illuminate all other moments. God lives in us, between us and around us.

Therefore, I told the priest, God should not be regarded as an answer to certain questions of science. God is not that which sets things in motion. God is that with which we are in communication in a continual creative process. In a sense, we make God, not God us. Or perhaps we make each other.

The priest seemed responsive to what I was saying. He said he hadn't really considered it before.

March 2

This afternoon I met a woman from Great Neck who was having lunch in a restaurant with a member of my congregation. There is a big dispute in her community about busing blacks into the school district and what she said to me crystallized the negative Jewish reaction. "Rabbi," she said, "we had to struggle to get out here, to make it for ourselves, and we have no intention of letting them take it away from us."

A rumor began circulating in our community last week that the busing of black students into our school district would be discussed at a school-board meeting. As a result, hundreds of angry white parents mobbed the meeting tonight, protesting hysterically, when the board never had any intention even of discussing the busing issue.

A reporter from the Long Island newspaper, *Newsday*, asked me to comment on this incident. My own feelings are that busing is destructive for the black community, because blacks would be better served if their own community life were strengthened. Removing them from their own structured life and putting them into white schools will only make them feel more inferior. However, since I'm not sure I've thought this through properly,

I didn't tell the reporter I opposed busing. Instead, I gave him some background to the problem.

The Jewish community in the Five Towns has grown layer upon layer, and although not apparent to most outsiders, the assimilation has been minimal. The major division is between the old guard and the newcomers, those who moved here before and those who moved here after the Second World War.

The old guard are the self-anointed people of quality, people with money but no stomach for flaunting it. They generally fall into two groups: the educated and the uneducated. The educated are the business executives and the professionals, doctors in the city and senior law partners in established firms in the city. The women dress simply and are active in various old-line charities; the children go to the best colleges; they themselves frequent the Philharmonic, the opera, and the theater. They also read books.

The second element in this old guard are the garment manufacturers, less assimilated than the educated old liners—many still have Yiddish dialects—and generally more Jewish in their identification. As a group, they are not cultivated, but they are good, sensitive people to whom the Jewish virtues of charity and humanity have always meant a great deal.

A middle group is made up of the thirty- and forty-year-old children of the old guard, who now live with their own families in the Five Towns. In a sense, they are modified old-liners, virtually all of them college-educated, assimilated, hard-working, and successful, if a bit more ostentatious than their parents. Through their parents, they have had enough contact with the old Jewish wisdom to carry on a certain humanity in their own lives.

The group that moved here since the Second World War is the archetype of Five Towners, those who have lost their Jewish humanity and haven't yet achieved their Anglo-Saxon polish. They are the nouveau riche, gaudy in their taste, who overdress, drive Cadillacs and Lincolns, and live generally to be noticed. Their overwhelming purpose in life seems to be only to outdo one another to be more like each other. The husband is typically a professional, although not well established, or the operator of a small business (usually soft goods—dresses, hats, etc.) in the city. The emphasis of this group is on spending money, often more than they have.

The old guard and the newcomers are as segregated from one another as they both are from the Gentiles. Each group is fairly self-contained, with its own country club, its own activities, its own synagogues, its own neighborhood.

The school district includes areas where both groups live, more established sections like Woodmere and the newer developments with $30,000 homes that all look alike, inside and outside. The hysterical parents at the school-board meeting tonight were the relative newcomers to the Five Towns, the ones who live in the new developments.

March 3

We have some men in Congress who are Jewish, but Herbert Tenzer, the man Allard Lowenstein succeeded last year, was a *Jewish* Congressman. What brings this to mind is a meeting of the Five Towns Coalition held tonight at which the point was raised that we would need furniture for a new health center the group is trying to get started in Inwood.

"Let's find out what we need," said Tenzer, "and then we'll all go around to each organization and ask them to contribute one desk or one lamp or one table. I'll give a desk. Rabbi, you give a table, and we can get this thing started."

If we had a Jewish President, there wouldn't have to be any taxes. We could have one great United American Appeal.

March 4

I received a call this evening from a very inactive member of my congregation, so inactive that after two years I have yet to meet him. He sends his children to be serviced at the religious school.

He called about the *Newsday* article in which I spoke of "the upward mobile people—those who have just moved in, find status in living here at the expense of very high mortgages and have a great fear of somebody taking it all away from them."

"I'm a member of your congregation, Rabbi," he said. "And I would like to know how you can say this trash? Anti-Semites are using this as the basis for their attacks against Jews."

March 5

A sixteen-year-old girl in the confirmation class, the daughter of a prominent member of the temple, hates me. Her father was one of my strongest supporters in bringing me here from Wheeling, but when she sees me she has such a fierce look in her eyes that I believe, given the opportunity, she would actually hit me. She is shrewd enough not to be blatant about her resentment, but she is very generous at throwing out hints.

Today when the class began, I remarked that very few students were present. "Last week everybody was here," she spoke up. "But that's only because you weren't."

Why she tries to hurt me personally like this baffles me, because I hardly know her. I imagine she probably hates me for some complex reason having to do with her father, and her feelings toward him. The rabbi has a built-in involvement in the lives of members of his congregation, and people are rarely neutral about him. There are cases, like this girl's, where he is the target of some very intense feelings which have nothing to do with him.

People tend to see the rabbi as a symbol for whatever they themselves are working toward, psychologically, emotionally, and intellectually. He is a scale on which they measure what they are, against what they would like to be. To the extent they fall short in their own self-esteem, they are likely to resent the rabbi. Conversely, if they think well of themselves, they think well of him. Therefore, what people think of me usually has nothing in fact to do with me. Most often, what they think of me only indicates what they think of themselves.

Perhaps, even though I hadn't thought about it, this is the reason I was so thrilled tonight when the worship committee adopted my suggestion for a temple-in-the-round in our temporary headquarters. The pulpit will be in the center of the floor, and the congregation will be praying with me, not at me.

March 6

The chairman of the nominating committee for the Five Towns Coalition today informed me that the group would like me to become its president. Since the coalition represents the first attempt by all voluntary organizations in the community to work together for social change, I was very pleased with the invitation, and knew immediately that I would accept it.

Of course I told them that I would think it over.

March 7

After a meeting of the worship committee today, a former president of the congregation asked me privately whether anybody has yet spoken to me about renewing my contract.

"No, nobody has," I said.

"Well, if you're satisfied, and we're satisfied, you ought to stay on," was his non-reply.

A few minutes later he and the current president, Bob Mandel, closeted themselves in a room for nearly an hour. When they emerged, neither of them said anything to me.

In spite of what their silence could mean, I decided today—finally—to have the swimming pool built in my yard. I want it in time for summer, I can afford it, and even if I leave the congregation or the rabbinate, I would like to continue living in this area. I called the contractor and told him to get started as soon as he could.

Judith and I have five house guests at the present—two nuns, a former priest, the former priest's wife, and their young child. The former priest, who is my age, and his family are staying with us until he finds a job. We've given them the third floor of the house, and they use the kitchen at certain specified times. We are able to coexist without constant contact.

The nuns, Eleanor Walker and Eva Fleischer, are members of the Grail, an organization of secular nuns—they do not wear habits and some of them are married—that could be called part of the liberal-radical wing of the Catholic Church. The group is centered in Grailville, Ohio, and last summer I attended a seminar there and was actually invited, as a rabbi, to participate in conducting a Mass. It was an informal Mass, in English, and I was very moved by the experience; I can think of a few American Cardinals who would be moved, too, probably to rage. Now I'm helping the Grail nuns set up a Jewish-Christian Institute for this summer.

In my own way, I'm deeply involved in Jewish-Christian relations, but I am ostracized from the establishment in that area. It's a complicated story. I have one link to the establishment, a nun, Sister Rose Thering, a Judophile of sorts, who always wears a pin inscribed SHALOM. Sister Rose works with Monsignor John Osterreicher, the head of the Institute of Jewish-Christian Studies at Seton Hall University. Monsignor Osterreicher is *the* Catholic expert on Jewish matters, presumably because long ago he was converted from Judaism to Catholicism. Austrian by birth, a stern man in his sixties or seventies, Osterreicher has spent most of his life zealously converting Jews to Catholicism.

Monsignor Osterreicher's counterpart among Jewish officialdom is Joseph Lichten, who specializes in Catholics for the Anti-Defamation League of B'nai B'rith. Not long ago, I went to see Lichten. I wanted him to help me set up more summer Jewish-Christian Institutes.

I could tell after the initial amenities that Lichten resented my intrusion into an area which he considered his own domain.

Early in our conversation, I made some frivolous, trivial remark—I don't even know exactly what it was—and he reacted as though I'd deeply offended him. He flew into a rage and practically shouted me out of his office. I was stunned. I didn't realize I was such a threatening figure.

As a result of this incident, neither Lichten nor his friend, Monsignor Osterreicher, nor any of their associates (except Sister Rose) will have anything to do with me. My Jewish-Christian Institute in Wheeling a few years ago was the first of its kind, but now I'm barred from official Jewish-Christian relations. I have to maintain my own.

March 8

As a guest speaker at today's services we had a young man, a recent Harvard graduate who is now studying to be a rabbi. He is also a member of a *Havurah,* a religious community where he and other rabbinical students pray, work, and study together.

He suggested that, since we live in an essentially unreligious atmosphere, a return to religion must come through communal living. He appealed for a Jewish underground church: community groups outside the decaying institutions where people will genuinely seek to learn together, rather than just go through the motions. The idea enthralls me. But the concept of the *Havurah,* he said—and this disturbs me—is that it is an attempt to merge Jewish authenticity with the qualities prevalent among today's radical youth.

I am disturbed because I feel that what radicals are doing today has no depth to it, only modness. When the style of the moment changes, whether it be Vietnam, black nationalism or environment, they change with it, using their freedom and dynamism to create a shadow anti-culture with virtually no substance around which a positive culture can collect. They are only raising their instincts to the level of values. There is nothing to hold it all together for them. They have no reference to the past, because they are more involved with liberating themselves from it than attempting to understand how they evolved from it and why. All we know of life is our experience as a human race in living it, but they live only immediately, glorifying their own values, and deceiving themselves into believing they are actually doing something *new*. It is not *new*. It has happened before. Many times.

Yet, remarkably, their instincts are often right, miraculously right. Unfortunately, the thin atmosphere in which they operate is doomed to evaporate, if only because they worship only themselves, and they are mortal.

Ironically, the personalism, the freedom, the individuality, and the creativity today's youth seems to be seeking are the backbone of the Jewish heritage. If only they could overcome their abhorrence of the past as simply a dead hand, Judaism could flourish as never before. Judaism was made for *now,* real Judaism, not $15,000-bar-mitzvah-Judaism. What we need is a delivery system, perhaps reverse *Havurahs,* means by which the kids could see that their insights are relevant, related to, in communication with and reflected off the 5,000-year experience of Judaism. Judaism can add the lacking dimension to today's youth culture. Like God, of course, Judaism is only a code word. The label is unimportant. It is merely meant to stand as a meaningful backdrop to our lives, as a symbol of our humility before the cosmos, as a larger context in which our little lives can function, as a realization that all we will ever know is not enough.

March 9

I watched an interview with Al Lowenstein on one of the TV shows yesterday.

I suppose he's become a very important person—the great white knight for the nation's young people. The interviewer asked him what motivated him, what kept him so busy, why youths always flocked around him, and I was surprised at Lowenstein's candor. He said that in his youth, he was always on the outside, always the different one, never really accepted, and that this had charged him with a very strong desire for recognition.

I admired his honesty. It was another facet of Lowenstein I had never seen. What he said was true: where there's a crowd, Al Lowenstein plays for adulation. Everybody has to be his best friend, and yet, I doubt he really has a single close friend. It seems he can only enter into human relationships on a certain level with celebrities or famous people whom he can admire or who can admire him. I keep remembering how strained he seemed when the two of us were together in my car driving to the temple. His conversation was so distant.

Today I told the nominating committee of the Five Towns Coalition that I would accept the presidency (or the chairmanship—I forget which it is) if I could have two co-chairmen (or vice-presidents), one of whom was black. They seemed responsive. The meeting is tomorrow.

Tonight I helped conduct a wedding in Temple Israel, followed by a reception in my favorite ballroom, beneath the glitter of its beautiful twinkling crystal chandelier. The bride's parents are active in my congregation and they insisted that I and the cantor conduct the wedding. Because we no longer have a building, they decided to hold the ceremony at Temple Israel. When they rented the room, they discovered a Temple Israel regulation: you automatically must hire the rabbi and the cantor. To complicate things even further, the mother also wanted the rabbi who had married her to participate in her daughter's ceremony. Grand total: three rabbis, two cantors and one million-dollar ballroom.

March 10

The *Times* this morning carried the wedding announcement, and it read as if I were the chief rabbi of a great cathedral with four assistants.

In the mail today I received a hate letter in response to my remarks quoted in *Newsday*. It was five single-spaced typewritten pages long, and accused me of being arrogant, negative, hostile and anti-Semitic, all in the first page. I didn't bother to read beyond.

Tonight I was elected chairman of the Five Towns Coalition, and the two co-chairmen I requested were also elected: Dick Nemith, a white man who owns a drug company, and John Kearse, a black man who is the executive director of the new Economic Opportunity Council and Community House.

March 11

In my class at Woodmere Academy this morning, I attempted to start a discussion about busing. A student interrupted me. "We don't want to hear about busing," he said. "We'd like to hear about Judaism for a change."

Even if the boy were right—and I see a connection between Judaism and busing—he could have found a kinder way to phrase his feelings.

In the afternoon, a gentleman came out from New York to have me sign an ad, titled "How New York's Jews Were Turned Against Black Men: Exploding the Myth of Black Anti-Semitism," which will be run on a full page in Sunday's New York *Times*. The ad is sponsored by a group calling itself the Jewish Citizens Committee for Community Control and will bear three signatures: Wendy Lehrman, chairman of the Jewish Teachers for Community Control; Larry Breakstone, Executive Board of the New Coalition Party and the United Federation of Teachers; and Martin Siegel, in my capacity as director of a formative group known as Rabbis for Community Control.

The text of the ad exposes the source of Jewish opposition to community control. "One agent, and one agent alone," it says, "initiated the campaign to concoct a fake threat of black anti-Semitism. That was the United Federation of Teachers [the teachers union]. Its intentions are transparent enough: the black anti-Semitism lie was the best means at hand to break the alliance between the liberal Jewish middle class and the black people of the city and so destroy the chances of school decentralization. . . .

"It [the UFT] is 'proving' to many that decentralization will pave the way for vicious vendettas against the Jewish schoolteachers of the city, a point the head of the UFT, Albert Shanker, has made from the start. Local control of the schools, he has frequently charged, 'would open up a field day for bigots.' "

The ad goes on to detail the complicity between the UFT and Jewish establishment organizations in weaving the black anti-Semitism myth, and reserves its most vituperative remarks for the Anti-Defamation League, "whose current stand on black anti-Semitism ('crisis-level') repudiates everything it has said before and does so with every cheap trick it can muster."

While the ad is angry and overwritten, the text is generally truthful, particularly in regard to the self-serving Jewish organizations which are almost totally removed from what I want Judaism to be. Since my only concern was with the style and not the substance of the ad, I asked the man if it could be toned down. He said it could not. He seemed adamant. I read it again, and felt very strongly that it needed the signature of a rabbi. For this reason, and because the ad's co-author is a man I trust, Walter Karp, a New York editor with whom I went to high school, I agreed to sign it.

March 12

A student at the Columbia Graduate School of Journalism who is doing a paper on Allard Lowenstein came out to interview me today, once again forcing me to re-evaluate this very complex man.

Earlier in the afternoon, I had spoken to Mrs. Lowenstein on the phone, and because she sounded like such a lonely woman, I had been thinking about the Congressman's forays around the world. One of his staff recently told me, perhaps apocryphally, that Lowenstein's wife once called Al and actually asked him to make an appointment to see his kids.

Unfortunately, the student asked me only for a political analysis of Lowenstein's situation, not a personal analysis. If he wanted a pundit, he shouldn't have come to a philosopher.

In the confirmation class this afternoon, I was discussing one of the most important concerns of human existence—the meaning of life and death. As the session drew on and I became more involved, I spotted the students checking their wrist-watches. When I was finished, they zipped right out. It was just another thing they were doing. Remarkable kids! I remember hearing about one of them who had asked his father to increase his allowance so he could contribute to his favorite causes. It must be wonderful to be an endowed radical.

At times like this, I wonder if I'm really getting anywhere. I'm just not sure. Nothing is really sure. There's so much doing and so little happening.

This year I am on more boards, more committees and more organizations than I can count. In addition, I'm doing this diary, two other books, soliciting for the Cornell Alumni Fund, and of course being rabbi, officiating at services, weddings, and funerals, preparing young men for their bar mitzvahs, and tending where I'm needed to the personal problems of members of the congregation. With all this, I sometimes wonder where I'm going! Am I doing anything for Judaism? In some small way am I preserving it? Making it meaningful to the future generation?

March 13

I had to go to the New York *Times* offices today because its advertising acceptability director was threatening to reject our ad. He considered portions of it libelous.

When I arrived, I met my colleagues for the first time. Almost all of them wore the tribal emblems of moustache and long hair and had a very distinctive East Village look. The advertising acceptability director, of course, was *Times* establishment, stable, reliable and responsible. He seemed relieved when I arrived. I don't have long hair and couldn't if I wanted to. Walter Karp, my high-school classmate, looked very intense. Although he had no moustache, he wore his hair very long and his eyes bore an unmistakably committed look. He and I may represent this new generation of Jews who are not hung up on anti-Semitism and want Judaism to be a movement for the improvement of society, not just for the Jews. I think we see this decentralization issue both as an attempt to make New York City into a livable place by sectioning it up into small communities and an effort to allow people more control in their own destiny.

There was terrific hostility from Walter and his group toward the *Times* man, because they felt the *Times* was partner to a conspiracy to hold up the ad while delicate negotiations over decentralization proceeded in Albany. Their reasoning appeared a bit paranoid to me. The man from the *Times* was really only insisting on toning down the language, especially with regard to Shanker, because of the possibility of libel. He was not asking that we remove the factual background of the argument.

My colleagues finally consented, and we were assured that the ad will run Sunday.

March 14

In this morning's mail, I got another reaction to my quoted remarks in *Newsday.*

Dear Rabbi Siegel:
Your quote was a pompous, patronizing way of castigating your own people. It seems to be open season on Jews this year. First, the New York City schools, then the UN, the Metropolitan Museum, Iraq, and now you.
Look at any district where they have busing. There is vandalism in the schools and there are Negroes beating up the white children. And you ask why we don't have busing here, while you sit on the pulpit and quote Maimonides and Charity.

I don't remember ever quoting Maimonides.

March 15

Today I learned that two and perhaps three couples in my congregation are getting divorced. One member of the temple board already had moved out of his house, and this was the first I had heard of it. In Wheeling, I doubt this could have occurred, at least not without my knowing and having a chance to help the persons involved work things out.

Here in the Five Towns a rabbi is not made to feel very welcome at getting involved in the lives of his congregants. If they're thinking about a wedding, they come to me. If they're thinking about a divorce, they go to a psychiatrist.

In Wheeling, we were a community (there are no more than 5,000 Jews in all of West Virginia), and we got involved in each other's lives. The town vibrated to births, marriages, and deaths. To this day, if I call a friend in Wheeling and ask what's happening, the answer will be that so-and-so is in the hospital, so-and-so is getting married, and so-and-so just had a baby. People care for one another.

My role as a rabbi in Wheeling was the more traditional one in terms of human involvement. I also served as an informal ambassador to the Gentiles. By virtue of my role as the rabbi of the leading temple in the community, there were memberships on various boards and committees in civic life. I was the official Jewish representative at everything from the DAR to the Historical Society. I served on the State Council on Arts and Humanities, the Clergy Council, the Rotary Club, even the faculty of a local Catholic college. My big business in Wheeling was delivering invocations and benedictions. No major occasion took place in the city unless I, along with a priest and a minister, did not give it my blessing.

Once, when the West Virginia Association of Real Estate Boards asked me to give the keynote address at a luncheon, I was so thrilled I titled my speech, "Up from Benedictions."

March 16

The ad was published this morning, and it was quite an imposing document—more words per square inch than I have ever seen, even in the New York *Times*.

Strangely enough, my phone didn't ring all day. I tried several times to call Bob Mandel (planning to mention another matter, but really to sense his reaction to the ad), but his line was busy every time I called. I assume he was getting the reaction I wasn't.

A few weeks ago, I received notice of a $50-a-plate fund-raising dinner for Al Lowenstein to be held tonight. I returned the card to indicate I planned to attend, but sent no money. I told one of his associates that I refused to pay for the dinner on the grounds that I worked for Lowenstein in the campaign. He sent a complimentary ticket.

Before the dinner tonight, I attended a reception given by former Congressman Tenzer at the Woodmere Country Club. Shortly after I arrived, Tenzer took me aside. He wanted me to spend as much time as I could with the guest speaker, a black man named Aaron Henry, a dentist who is the head of Mississippi's NAACP and Freedom Democratic Party. "He's been critical of rabbis in Mississippi," Tenzer told me, "and I'd like to show him that all rabbis are not like Mississippi rabbis." So I was brought in as Exhibit A, Nice Liberal Rabbi, to Dr. Henry for the evening. In spite of this we had a very interesting conversation, mainly on religion.

At the dinner later, during the speeches, Representative Ogden Reid quoted a newspaper story in which being a friend of Lowenstein was likened to being perpetually on the hold button of a telephone. I rather liked that. Lowenstein got around to giving his speech very late, and he limited his remarks to quoting Robert Kennedy, one of his heroes.

Throughout the evening, Rabbi Sandrow was sitting at a nearby table and making somewhat cluckingly negative remarks about the *Times* ad. I don't think he knew I heard him, and later as we were leaving, he spotted me and waved.

"Hello, Martin."

"Hello," I answered.

"Martin, I'd like to talk to you. Did you sign that ad?"

"Yes."

"Well, Martin, perhaps we'll talk about it sometime."

March 17

This evening I was summoned to the luxurious East 69th Street townhouse of Mr. and Mrs. Arthur Krim, local power magnates, to help organize support for community control. I arrived a few minutes early and the servants told me that the Krims had not yet returned from their previous cocktail party. I snooped around while I waited and two things struck me as rather excessive: their home had more marble than a museum, and more photos of Lyndon Johnson than must be hanging in all of Johnson City. Mr. Krim, who is the president of United Artists, is one of the chief fund-raisers for the Democratic Party.

When the Krims finally arrived, they were accompanied by Mr. and Mrs. Whitney Young. I used to consider Whitney Young, the president of the Urban League, *the* Negro statesman.

A few other people attended, but none was as notable as Young. Mrs. Krim, a quiet, intelligent woman with a foreign background, impressed me because she seemed most committed to the community-control cause. In fact, it appeared as if her husband had taken up the issue because of her interest.

To me, the most interesting aspect of the evening was the relationship between Whitney Young and his wife. He, very sympathetic to community control and school decentralization, spent much of the evening elaborating, as if talking to Lyndon Johnson, on why he supported these issues. Mrs. Young, however, is much more conservative, and at one point in the discussion she interrupted her husband's argument.

"Whitney," she demanded. "Are the blacks ready for this kind of power? Or are you just trying to give it to them whether they are ready or not?"

Mrs. Young struck me as a black aristocrat. She reminded me of a friend of mine, a fellow from Atlanta who was with me during the late 1950s on a student tour of Russia carefully arranged by the State Department. He was our Black Face and all questions about the racial situation in the United States, which intrigued the Russians, were, of course, directed at him. "Let me tell you about my case," he would say. "I live in a $75,000 home. We have three cars and white servants. I go to Columbia University and my sister goes to Barnard. Would you call that discrimination?"

The first time Mrs. Young interrupted her husband, he ignored her. But she persisted, almost antagonistically. "Why should white people do anything for the blacks, Whitney?" she said. "We don't need their help. We should do it ourselves."

"Dear," he answered, "please keep quiet. This is not what you should be concerned about. You are destroying the direction of the conversation."

"Oh Whitney, don't get so excited," she said.

"Shut up and keep quiet, dear," said Young to his wife.

March 18

A lady this afternoon told me she was very worried about me because of Sunday's ad in the *Times*. From what she heard, she said, the temple could be losing up to a hundred members because of me.

I had her remark on my mind when I attended a regularly scheduled meeting of the board of trustees of the temple in the evening. We met in the old building; it's being dismantled, but there was just enough left of it to hold the meeting there. The stripped walls and hanging wires provided a very appropriate atmosphere for the bleak confrontation I expected and got.

I had no sooner come through the door than the religious-school director stopped me and said she had received five calls about the ad, all negative. Before the meeting, Bob Mandel told me that his phone had been ringing all day Sunday with a series of negative, sometimes vituperative, calls. He was angry with me because I had not told him in advance about the ad. Actually, I had told him, but I had been less than explicit. I do think he probably had a right to be angry, because I *did* know he would be put out by the affair, and the least I could have done was to have forewarned him.

In spite of my lack of consideration, Mandel handled the callers in a manner I had to appreciate. He told each of them that "the rabbi" had signed the ad as a private citizen and that Temple Sinai was not mentioned at all. "Since the rabbi makes no pretense to represent the temple," he told them, "he has a right to put his name where he wants it." I regarded this as very magnanimous on his part because I knew he disagreed with some of the contentions raised in the ad.

The most fortunate thing about the ad, as it turns out, was its length. Most people didn't bother to read through it. If they had, the reaction might have been even more severe. After all, our community raises a good deal of money for the Anti-Defamation League.

In the course of the meeting itself, the subject of the ad was never brought up, but we had a substitute symbol. We had been forwarded a series of resolutions to vote on prior to a convention of the New York State Federation of Reform Synagogues, and one of the resolutions dealt with black-Jewish relations. The tenor of this resolution was very holier-than-thou: it made the point that *in spite* of the rise in black anti-Semitism, which has created the current situation, we as Jews are not going to turn against the blacks.

I obviously had to object, because the resolution conceded a rise in black anti-Semitism when I feel that this is all an invention of the teachers union and the ADL to serve their own self-interest. The very term black anti-Semitism presupposes a black community which doesn't exist. With no real unity and no real leadership, they are just a group of individuals who are only slowly gaining a sense of cohesiveness, a sense of belonging to one another. The Jews have been a community for 4,000 years—they have the structure to react to anti-Semitism. What they don't seem to understand is that the blacks don't have the cohesiveness to be communally anti-Semitic.

Fortunately for me, I had an ally, a man who is the news director at an all-news radio station, WINS, in New York. He eloquently questioned the authenticity of the resolution. I only seconded him.

Bob Mandel disagreed with us. He supported the resolution because he felt that black anti-Semitism did pose a threat to the Jews. He felt so strongly that he relinquished the chair.

I said to him that our disagreement was partly semantic. I said I didn't deny the rise in black militancy—that's a fact—I just denied the rise in black militancy as a result of black anti-Semitism. This only seemed to make matters between us worse.

"I have a lot of friends who teach in the schools," Mandel said. "And simply because they are Jews, Rabbi, they have had a hard time with the blacks. That's a fact, Rabbi."

As we both strained to be polite, someone motioned that we table the resolution until the next meeting. This was passed, 8 votes to 4, and I was pleased because, had it come to a showdown, one of us, obviously, would have been a loser. It is better not to have this kind of special confrontation between me and the president. I don't think it's good for the congregation. Or me.

March 19

Construction began today on our long-awaited pool, which, because it represents to me a decision to remain in this community, came at a very unpropitious time. I have been informed that three couples have resigned from the congregation because of me, and it looks like more resignations will follow. Each of the members who resigned was extremely fearful of black anti-Semitism, and my signature on the ad Sunday seemed to precipitate their decision. If for no other reason than that the congregation—with the building project—is financially overcommitted and seeking to increase its membership, I think the resignations are going to hurt.

Strange as it may seem, nobody has approached me directly about the ad. The disgruntled members have gone directly to the president, with my undoing foremost in their minds. There has always been some well-entrenched opposition to me for my views on religion, and now these people, in alliance with my recently inspired opposition, may make the going very difficult. The woman in one of the couples who resigned is a teacher in the religious school who, although not an active member of the congregation, has been lobbying for my removal ever since her husband and I had a large disagreement over Vietnam. The argument was touched off when I encouraged last year's confirmation class to write part of their own confirmation service, and they did, devoting a portion of it to antiwar discussion. She and her husband would have preferred it had I censored the service. Today, in their letter of resignation, they complained that since my tenure as rabbi began, "The direction of the congregation has been to the left, which we do not find to our liking."

I myself find these resignations very useful, quite frankly, for weeding out those in our congregation who didn't belong in the first place. I don't think the congregation can move into the exciting new experiments I have in mind if it is weighted down by the kind of people who get upset because the rabbi—as a free agent—signs an ad in the New York *Times* outlining how black anti-Semitism has been so greatly exaggerated.

On the other hand, this overreaction to my activities really disturbs me, not so much because it may forbode the end to my days as a rabbi, but because of what it could mean in terms of my synagogue's willingness to cope with the last vestiges of authentic Judaism. Unlike the Christian denominations, and especially Catholicism, where rigid hierarchy assures unity through uniformity, the genius of Judaism is that it has achieved its own unity without ever demanding uniformity. Unlike the church, the smallest unit of Jewish worship—the synagogue—is virtually autonomous. Synagogues answer only to their congregations.

There are many synagogues—like Temple Israel in this community—which cannot be considered a serious measure of the survival of authentic Judaism. I myself could never survive at Temple Israel or any of the temples, scattered coast to coast, of that type. I would have been thrown out a long time ago. In fact, I would have never been hired.

But Temple Sinai is precisely where Judaism should be preserving its great heritage of unity without uniformity. Conformity has never been a virtue in this congregation. We have always highly valued the individual. The institution itself has always been a forum, a place to *exchange* our attitudes. We have never permitted it to *prescribe* our attitudes.

But what is happening now? It seems that simply because I have spoken out—not in the temple's name, but in my own, for something in which I genuinely believe—I am threatened. What hope does this leave modern Judaism? Where do we go if a synagogue like Temple Sinai decides it cannot tolerate a rabbi who asks only for the right to think for himself?

March 21

Now that I am also getting persecuted, the cantor is being especially kind to me. We are both acting like employees, and have found a common recreation in grumbling. In this sense, I imagine, we are like keypunch operators for IBM.

After the service today, we had this exchange:

Cantor: "Did you see Forst? He was sneering all through the service."

Rabbi: "No, but I couldn't tell the difference if I did. He was born sneering."

Cantor: "He's got a small mind, anyway."

Rabbi: "I know. I can't believe he's so rigid. Sometimes I think he's nothing but a grown-up Boy Scout."

Cantor: "Mrs. Goldberg said the *Mi Hamocha* was too slow."

Rabbi: "What does she know about Jewish music?"

Cantor: "Nothing. She's a big pain in the neck."

Rabbi: "And always looking to find fault."

Cantor: "What did you think of Eisenberg today?"

Rabbi: "He's always so involved with himself. So selfish. He always seems to need recognition."

Cantor: "Another grown-up Boy Scout."

Despite the conversation, there is one major difference between the cantor and me: he hates the congregation congenitally; I'm just piqued.

March 22

A member of my confirmation class brought me an interesting piece of gossip today. "You know what my parents said about you, Rabbi?" he told me. "They said you're a rabbinical Sammy Glick, that you really like material things and that you want them even more than they do. And they said the way you justify yourself is by constantly attacking others who have material things, which just proves your desire to have them."

With a swimming pool under construction in my back yard, I could not very easily dismiss what he said, and I spent a good part of the day thinking about it. I still feel, however, that while I do like to have certain *things,* which—true—those people I criticize also like to have, I consider them secondary and relatively unimportant. I like to live well, but if principle were at stake, I would give up any of the *things* I now have. There's nothing depraved about wanting to live comfortably; it's only when this dominates the life-style and becomes the standard for fulfillment that something is dreadfully wrong.

It's idolatrous to have *things* as the center of value.

I was forced to pick up the same subject later in the day in a conversation with Bob Mandel, who told me that I was turning off a large group of the young married couples in the congregation because of my unrelenting sermons on the unvalue of worshipping material things.

One of my consistent themes, in sermons and in private conversations, is that in having no otherworldly or external God at their disposal these days, many people are making the *things* they collect their trophies of life's accomplishments. The president told me that some members told him they are tired of being attacked. "They don't want to hear all the time how bad it is to have material things," he said. Mandel himself seemed neutral, but he was obviously concerned that it would be bad for business if I insisted on continuing to say these things.

He also brought up the difference of opinion we had at the board meeting, but said only that "perhaps" I should not be a delegate to the New York Federation of Reform Synagogues Convention because my views did not represent the congregation's on the black anti-Semitism issue.

I might have pursued the point, but he changed the subject to the question of my future tenure, and said that it was his opinion that the majority of the congregation stood behind me, and that I had more supporters than detractors, including him. He vowed that if there were any problem with regard to my tenure, he would resign. I admitted I was surprised, but quite pleased by his support. He said he was setting up a small committee to negotiate with me.

Mandel has been reading Herbert Tarr's book, *Heaven Help Us*, a novel about a rabbi and his congregation. He told me he finds the book very funny. I don't. At the end, the rabbi gets fired.

March 23

This morning I was not very well received in some classes at the religious school. A few of the teachers work full-time in the public schools in the city, and because of the ad last Sunday, I felt they were very hostile to me.

March 24

I am in the process of setting up four major committees in the congregation: social action, adult education, youth liaison, and community relations. Now that the decision to put up the building has been made, I would like the congregation to start thinking about something worthwhile to put into it. Of course, some of them are already thinking about putting a new rabbi in it.

March 25

We moved the temple offices into a small suite above the firehouse in Lawrence today. My first visitor in the new quarters was a twenty-five-year-old black man named Jim Deleston who is running for a seat on the school board and wants my support. Even though there are at least 300 blacks in the schools, there has never been a black on the board.

Deleston is obviously not used to dealing with whites, and I noticed a sternness in his face that was either fear or hatred. Because he was extremely polite—too polite—I decided later that he was simply scared.

"Rabbi Siegel," he said. "I believe we need black representation on the school board, and I am the one who can do it."

"I agree we need black representation," I said, "but why you?"

"Your point is well taken," he said. "I am the most qualified candidate." He was very nervous.

As our conversation progressed, I began to feel that he

really wasn't very qualified or capable, and this created a serious dilemma. On principle, I wanted a black representative on the board. He didn't have to be *qualified* by white standards, but he did have to be able to cope with the work. I wasn't sure if Deleston could. Of course, my support doesn't mean much, but it does mean a little. A number of kids who know Deleston is running have already asked me whether I will work for his election; so have a number of adults.

When Deleston left, I phoned some friends in the black community. I asked them if they had anybody other than the twenty-five-year-old to run for the seat. In effect, they said Deleston was all they had. Take him or leave him.

I decided that if I am going to make an error I want to err on the side of helping the blacks. I've seen standards too often become excuses for white racism. Blacks must be brought into the governing process, and if, in the interim, we suffer a dilution in the quality of our public officials, in the long run we are building toward a more just and fair society. For these reasons, I decided to support Deleston.

March 28

After officiating at a funeral this morning, I came back to our temporary temple at the Masonic Temple for a rehearsal for a special service to be conducted tonight by the Men's Club. The tradition is that we always rehearse these things for fear the service will be lacking professionalism. Tomorrow we will have a mother-daughter Sabbath, and we had a rehearsal for that, too.

Imagine: we rehearse to pray.

March 29

The mother-daughter service this morning was a sell-out. Hundreds of people couldn't find a place to sit except the floor.

There is a reason for the turnout. It happens every time we have any program involving children. People today have moved away from an external God, yet really aren't satisfied with just worshipping themselves, primarily because they realize they don't stand for anything except their Cadillacs and Puccis. Thus the children, because they provide all the things God used to provide (immortality, love, relationship, etc.), have been moved in to become the center of value, the living idols.

March 30

Two weeks to the day after the fact, they arrived. Two men from the Anti-Defamation League. *Local representatives,* dispatched by the national organization. One, a former leader of the local chapter, was a man mystically attached to the ADL because it had helped his son get into medical school. The other was a man from my congregation. It was a transparently worked-out strategy, which I understand is the result of a recent regional meeting in which much of the discussion was taken up with the problem of what to do about me.

The member of my congregation (he is one of a few people who are acting like industrial spies and helping the ADL to compile a dossier on me) kept referring to himself as an *indignant* member of my congregation. I'm sure that in his indignation the

ADL meant for me to see that my own position was in jeopardy, that therefore I should retreat from my stand on community control.

It's a shame that the ADL has become so self-involved and so defensive that it can't honestly admit a mistake. The organization is torn by institutional schizophrenia: creating black anti-Semitism where it didn't exist and then standing adamant against community control on the grounds that it would lead to more strident black anti-Semitism. Prior to this, they had been one of the leading Jewish organizations interested in building communication with the blacks. Of course, even then communication meant dealing alternately with Whitney Young and Roy Wilkins, the "official" leaders of the blacks. Then, when the *real* black leaders began demanding that we give something up, the ADL quickly shifted its stance from liberal to conservative. Like many Jews, it was forced into conservatism because it suddenly had something to conserve. In Judaism, there has always been this conflict between the prophet and the priest—between those who wanted change and those who wanted to preserve. Today we have the young people who are prophetic, while the old choose to stand by and guard their empty cathedrals.

The meeting lasted for two hours and accomplished nothing. They didn't come to listen and I have listened enough to them. They had come with the predisposition that the ADL was the closest thing to the Jewish Papacy, and they found me dangerously heretical because I passed the time overstating how much I really despised them. They accused me of abetting anti-Semitism and I accused them of using cheap tricks. I did finally offer to bring my group, Rabbis for Community Control, to meet their group, and they said they would relay the word to Above.

Later in the day a man from the American Jewish Congress also called and said he wanted to meet with me. Perhaps this is the greatest thing the ad accomplished. It had made the Jewish establishment aware that there *is* opposition. Our purpose is to show them that there is a significant group inside the Jewish community which favors community control and is not opposed to the blacks and is willing to see some Jewish interests sacrificed for the sake of justice for the blacks.

This evening a nineteen-year-old girl I met two weeks ago at a wedding came to see me because she wants to convert to Judaism. When I asked her to read some books by Martin Buber, she broke down and cried. "I don't understand Martin Buber," she said.

Of course, her inability to understand Martin Buber was not the real reason she cried. The girl had been under psychiatric care before she got married; then she found security in her husband. But since the marriage, her in-laws have become an increasingly dominating force. Her husband, she has found, is both economically and emotionally dependent on his parents. Now the in-laws want her to convert, and they are using their position as a billy club. They have three sons and they want to make her a daughter. She can't understand Martin Buber, and therefore in her mind she can't become a daughter to her husband's parents, and therefore his source of strength—and hers—will be cut off.

At the moment, she is in a very bad way. She claims that everything her husband says makes her nervous.

The circumstances are familiar to me because they are a recurring problem in many Jewish families. The girl the son marries is brought into the family as another sibling, and the marital relationship is thwarted, never allowed to develop naturally. It's as if brother married sister. The whole situation reeks of emotional incestuousness. I was involved in a similar situation once where the wife couldn't find a role for herself and constantly related to her husband's parents instead of her own. Ultimately, she was driven to suicide.

With this in mind, I told the young girl tonight that she would not have to read Martin Buber. I usually tailor the conversion preparation to meet the needs of the individual, anyway.

If the person to be converted is bright, I have him read Buber and other intellectual books which provide a depth of understanding. If not, I use some of the more basic textbook-type volumes. I encourage all potential converts to attend services, and to study the practice of Judaism, the traditions and the holidays. In what turns out to be basically a tutoring course, I give them assignments, and we have discussions on them. The process takes, on the average, three or four months.

March 31

I conducted a funeral this morning for a man who forty years ago had been given up for dead, but survived, and even though he lost his business, built another one and died a very wealthy man. In the eulogy, I tried to express what the family felt for him. I simply tried to verify their feelings, without exaggerating and without rambling. As I was getting into the car to go to the cemetery, the widow took me by the arm and said, "Rabbi, I couldn't have said it better myself. I'll always remember the way you put it and what you said."

A funeral is never easy for me. I hate to see people grieved; I hate to see them hurt; I hate to see them confronted with the reality of permanent absence. I always try to comfort those who feel the loss most heavily and are trying to adjust to it. Everything I do—the way I act, what I say—is intended to help sow the seeds of recovery. Sometimes this is a problem, because people want to be assured there is life after death, even though Judaism is not a salvation system. We don't live for death and we don't promise an afterlife, but because there is nothing concrete in the religion precluding it, I usually fudge the point when people who are under stress persist for an answer.

I am often asked to officiate at funerals for people I never knew. Because of the emotional drain on me, I usually turn these down. There are some rabbis who do as many funerals as they can. Like weddings, funerals can be a business, and for a rabbi willing to free-lance regularly, the extra cash can be considerable. Although never formally stated, it's understood that a rabbi gets between $50 and $100 per funeral or wedding.

Since I don't want to feel that I'm operating on a fee-for-service basis, I never allow money to become a consideration in whether I conduct a funeral.

I can't say the same about weddings. There have been occasions when I have done weddings for the money alone. This usually occurs when I discover that the people involved are so selfish and self-concerned that money is the only compensation I have.

I don't often feel this way, but an incident occurred shortly after I came to Temple Sinai which still lingers bitterly in my mind. A couple who were not members of my congregation came to see me about marrying their daughter. They had assorted problems—the usual ones, such as juggling the caterer and the marriage palace with the date, and I spent a good deal of time helping them work things out. The father of the bride was a dentist who lived two blocks from me.

After much trouble, I arranged the ceremony and conducted the wedding, yet they never paid me or even invited me to the reception. In fact when the ceremony was over, they simply walked off, and never said thank you, or even *Good-bye, Charlie.*

For months afterward, I seriously contemplated sending them a bill.

After today's funeral, I went to New York to attend a meeting of the Coalition for Community Control, an amalgamation of groups from the Junior League to the League of Women

Voters, most of them women-oriented, do-good and WASPish. Only one black attended and, as far as I could tell, I was the only Jew.

The group had done a good deal of research into the legislative possibilities of decentralization in various forms, and had developed its position around three basic stances: community control of finances, community appointment of teachers and community control of curriculum, conceding only a few "cosmetic" points to placate Albert Shanker and the union.

I fully supported them, because all these reforms, in my mind, are designed to improve the quality of education and to improve the quality of life in the city. The improvement of the human condition, which community control will hopefully help to accomplish, is a Jewish imperative, even though for the moment Jews don't seem to realize the connection.

I realize it because I have lived outside New York City for many years and have watched small communities operate. To see the quality of life where people are not brutalized by being forced together in large competitive units, where people don't have to fight for every breath of fresh air, every inch of space, is exhilarating. The people of New York should be given the same chances.

April 1

The builder poured the cement for my pool this morning.

Still no word from the temple about my contract. Apparently, they're either reconsidering because of the ad two weeks ago, or trying to make me think they're reconsidering because of the ad two weeks ago.

In the evening, the executive committee of the Five Towns Coalition met in my home. We spent most of the time giving direction to our subcommittees—housing, race relations, membership, personnel, practices for domestics and, inevitably, public relations.

John Kearse, one of the co-chairmen, objected when somebody suggested we take a stand for building the proposed Nassau expressway. He felt that we were formed as an agency to assist the disadvantaged and that concerning ourselves with expressways would be a dissolution of our efforts. One of the traditional problems of do-good agencies is that they attempt to do good for everybody and ultimately do little good for anybody. Therefore, we decided not to take a stand on the expressway issue. It was a significant decision for us because it congeals our commitment to what we established ourselves for.

April 2

Judith, Sally and I had our own Passover seder tonight, and I thought back to the first seder I can recall, one conducted by my grandfather, who told of the evil Pharaoh of Egypt, brave Moses, and the final victory of the Jews over the Egyptians. As I was glorying in "our victory," my grandfather ended the ceremony by announcing to all, "Next year in Jerusalem."

Each person at the table then turned to his neighbor and repeated with great enthusiasm, "Next year in Jerusalem." I was so confused that I turned to my grandfather and said, "Next year, what in Jerusalem?"

He gave me a typical Jewish grandfather answer: "My dear grandson, when you are a little older you will understand."

April 4

Tonight was the night for the Sermon of the Year, the great crowd-pleaser, the drawing card. I spoke about Philip Roth's novel, *Portnoy's Complaint,* a very explicit account of a young man's attempt to liberate himself through sexual exploits from a *Jewish* childhood.

The turnout was staggering. I saw faces in the congregation I hadn't seen since last Yom Kippur and, if it hadn't been for Roth's Jewish-book-to-end-all-Jewish-books, might not have seen again until next Yom Kippur. Everybody came to hear the Word from the Rabbi on this surreal character of the Jewish experience, Alexander Portnoy. Even my mother drove out from Brooklyn.

My mother seemed to be a little nervous when she arrived, and pulled me aside before the service began. She had just read the book. "That Mrs. Portnoy," she said, "she was a wonderful mother."

"Yes, Mother," I said.

"After all, Martin," she said, "she was only doing what was best for her children."

I chose the topic for two reasons: first, because I sensed an overwhelming demand from the congregation; second, I know I'm in the religious wing of show business. It's not unusual for members of my congregation to check the sermon announced in the temple newsletter against the *Cue* listings before they choose between the synagogue and the movies. What better way, I thought, to compete with *I Am Curious* (*Yellow*) than to sermonize on *Portnoy's Complaint?*

I began my sermon by attempting to show the circumstances out of which Portnoy grew, and this took me back briefly to Eastern Europe around the turn of the century. Religion was a very meaningful force in the lives of the Jews who lived in the ghetto communities, something that held them together intellectually, spiritually and practically as they struggled to exist in their condition of appalling poverty. The men and the women in these communities each had their own generally accepted roles. The men worked, of course, but they drew their real status from scholarly pursuits, often connected with the *Talmud.* Learning, scholarship and religiosity were a way of life for them, the substance of their manhood. On the other hand, the women took on a more practical role; they managed the daily affairs of the family, cooking, cleaning, and administering the meager income. In the early part of the twentieth century, the great migration of these Jews from Eastern Europe to America took place, prompted by local pogroms, increasing discrimination, and liberal immigration laws in the United States.

When the Jews arrived in America, the sudden, radical change of environment instantly upset the traditional family balance. Survival, which in the familiar environs of Europe was a way of life, became a preoccupation in America. The man's status as a scholar became irrelevant, and he was forced into the new, unsatisfying role of working long hours with little, if any, time remaining for his intellectual passions. On the other hand, the mother, with her very practical abilities, became the logical one to keep the family together and supervise the adjustment to the new environment. Thus, at the same time the mother grew more and more overbearing, the father was losing his sense of masculine purpose.

The children were a blend of their mother's pragmatism, which they were able to experience in operation, and their father's intellectual inclinations, which had never been fully transplanted to America. Father drilled son with a respect for knowledge and learning, and the son accumulated the technical and intellectual skills which allowed him to move upward in American society.

But unlike the father, the son glorified his education as a means to a social end. In Europe, where there was virtually no social mobility for Jews, the father pursued knowledge out of a religious and moral impulse. The son never realized the connection between what he learned and what he, as a human, could never know. To him, scholarship was another abstract virtue, which had nothing to do with Judaism. Also, because of confusion of his father's role, he carried the residual problem of dealing with his own masculinity.

Thus Alexander Portnoy grew up as a Jew without Judaism, without any relationship to God, without any moral standards. The product of a dominant mother and an emasculated father, he is the son who in an external sense wants to do good (What was he? New York's Commissioner of Human Relations), but who is internally so afflicted with confused moral standards that he is without ability to discipline himself.

Portnoy did some very grotesque things, not because, as he may have thought, he was liberated, but because he couldn't cope with the real beauty of sex, its aesthetic harmony. That would involve relationship. Portnoy could only cope with gratification.

In fact, Portnoy *sought* gratification to *avert* relationship. He degraded himself and his women, one of whom he called "Monkey," into animals, and the two of them, without any involvement, mutually exploited one another in sexual encounters so bizarre they were beyond most people's fantasies. Any attempt to broaden, or deepen, his relationships failed.

I am not a prude. I just happen to find the whole intrigue of life in human relationships, not in sexual intercourse alone.

It is not that Portnoy did not have feelings. He did. But he projected his concern for human involvement into the abstract reality of doing good for all society, while he himself remained incapable of entering into real human relations. His intellectual revelations were one thing, his human existence another. Unlike his father, he had not been conditioned to operate in a context in which the two could relate.

While encouraging scholarship, Judaism essentially speaks in relationships. Gratification is selfish, but in relationship there is mutual concern, mutual fulfillment. This was at the basis of

Portnoy's anguish. Probably because of his residual Jewish qualities, the pleasure he pursued was not pleasurable. He couldn't believe in it, and yet he suffered from a confused masculine role which demanded it.

After the sermon there was a hearty response from the congregation. In the street, a doctor, zooming by in his fancy sports car, screeched to a halt. "I really enjoyed the sermon," he shouted from the window.

My mother, incidentally, went back to Brooklyn relieved. "Martin, dear," she said, "I'm glad you weren't too hard on us."

April 5

The other day, I saw the cantor on the street. He seemed to be thinking deeply about something.

"I only have one thing to say to you," he said to me. "And that is if I have to go, I'm going to be taking a lot of people with me."

"Listen," I said, "all I care about from you is that you don't make any trouble for me. I don't care what you do in your business life or your personal life. I'm just sick and tired of arguing with you all the time. Just do your job, and nobody cares what you do."

He phoned me today and said he had something wrong with his mouth and he couldn't work, which left me to do the singing at the service. I was awful. The congregation certainly missed the cantor today.

April 6

I had a visit today from the parents of an eleven-year-old girl who has been caught shoplifting small items at local stores. The parents have already taken her, without success, to a psychologist and a psychiatrist, and they are now beginning to feel very hopeless about her.

I think what they fail to see is the degree to which they are part of her problem. For one thing, they are both very active in leftist political causes, and they simply don't have much time to give her attention. But, even more importantly, I sensed that the wife really doesn't care that much about her. Both she and her husband were previously married, and the girl is the product of the husband's first marriage. The woman is angry at her husband's first wife, and she sees in the girl some of the things she dislikes about her mother. Therefore, in her subtle antagonism, she seems to encourage the girl's antisocial behavior.

When I told the wife this, she was defensive. "I'm not sure I agree with you, Rabbi," she said. "She is my husband's daughter and I do love her."

"You make it sound like an obligation," I said.

She had no answer.

I told her that I felt the best way she could help the child was to develop a genuine feeling for her. Right now, she is threatening to send her away to school, which is no substitute for the warmth she needs.

This past weekend was the second anniversary of the death of my father. Even though it's customary to go to the cemetery, I spoke, instead, at a memorial service for Martin Luther King, where I pleaded for black-white understanding.

I think my father would agree that it was more important for me to do something useful for the living than to pay obeisance to an ancestor. He was a very gentle man. I think of him often. Like Mr. Portnoy, he was moderately successful (he was an accountant), but he found it very difficult to find a role for himself. My mother was the dominant figure in the family. He always seemed so shy toward me. The last thing he said to me was, "Martin, we're going to have a long talk someday."

We never did.

April 7

At a conference on black anti-Semitism at a Methodist church today, a black man in an Afro costume made a very interesting point. He said Black Power is only an interim ethic which will eventually be succeeded by a more mature point of view.

"Yes," I told him, "but in the meantime, we have to expect a more intelligent reaction from the black community to its own self-interest. The blacks must see that the charges of anti-Semitism are hurting them, and they should do all they can to denounce the misconception that they are anti-Semitic. This would open up the way for a real dialogue."

"Who are you to tell me we should make an intelligent response?" he shouted at me.

That was the end of our dialogue.

I didn't mean any harm, but he reacted to me as if I were just another do-good white liberal Jew. He refused to listen to me. The conference proceeded from there: the whites didn't listen to the blacks and the blacks didn't listen to the whites and the Christians didn't listen to the Jews and the Jews didn't listen to the Christians.

An interesting sidelight occurred when a Black Panther

made a rather bizarre appeal for contributions to the Panther legal fund. "Man," he said, "if you don't give us what we want, we're going to take it. Violence is the only way you can get anything in this society, and we're gonna be violent."

A lot of black aggression, of course, is only verbal frustration. But I'd rather have them yelling at us than shooting at us.

I gave a dollar.

April 8

A busy day in the God business:

When I arrived at my office this morning, a secretary greeted me, most improbably, "Good morning, Rabbi, I've been thinking about God."

"Oh," I said.

"I don't think I really believe in the formal God," she insisted. "I like being Jewish, but I don't see this God thing at all. I believe in the ethic and the identity of Judaism."

"You have to ask yourself what you don't believe in," I answered. "Are you rejecting a concept or are you rejecting the whole God reality? Your concept of God is unimportant. The only thing that should matter is your own personal relationship to God."

It was the best I could do before I had my coffee.

A few minutes later, a woman I'd never seen appeared in my office. She had some questions about God, she said. Her daughter had begun to doubt God's existence and she wanted some information to answer her back with. I gave her two hour's worth of God information.

In the evening, ten minutes before the start of the service for the last day of Passover, none of the congregation had yet appeared. The three hired hands—the cantor, the organist, and I—were chattering in the lobby when a man with a briefcase, who had just rushed off the train, burst through the door.

He looked at us. "What are you fellas waiting for?" he said. "The Messiah to come? You should be ready. You should be in your robes."

We gave him what he'd ordered—a one-man service.

April 9

A lady in the congregation asked me today if my diary would have an index when it was published.

"Why do you want to know?" I asked.

"Because I want to know if I'll have to read through the stuff about God before I find the part about me," she said.

April 10

I met this morning with a boy who will celebrate his bar mitzvah this week. "What do you think you'll be doing when you become a man?" I asked him.

"Probably fighting for my country," was his reply.

The thought depressed me. Saturday, as a Jew, he will come

of age reading from the moral law. In a few years, he will enter American Manhood by fighting in the army.

In the evening, I attended a board meeting of the Community House, which decades ago, when this community was a haven for the Four Hundred, was founded by Mrs. Russell Sage as a trade school for the children of the servants in the area. Over the years, it has turned into a settlement house–recreation center for the blacks. Because it recently merged with the government-sponsored poverty agency, the board is a strange amalgamation of society types, semi-intellectual and semi-leftist Jews, black militants, and black Toms.

Naturally, with a cast of characters like this, the board is tangled in its own labyrinth of attitudes, which range from the old-style social welfare to the new-style black self-determination. The executive director is John Kearse, who headed the poverty agency before the merger, my co-chairman on the Five Towns Coalition. Tonight he proposed five half-day sessions in which we board members would get to know about the Community House and one another. The board resolutely turned him down. "I want to help the poor," one of the members told me, "but I can't afford to spend that much time doing it."

The meeting was as unwieldy as the composition of the board. I recalled for them my experience on the old board before the merger, when we had spent hours haggling over such vital matters as whether or not we would sponsor a dance, where, when, and who would address the envelopes, who would stamp the envelopes, who would send them out. I told them that now as a merged group we had a budget of nearly half a million dollars, and it was time we rose above the trivia. Everybody agreed.

When I left at eleven, halfway through the agenda, they were in an involved debate over where and when the next meeting would be held.

April 14

I sometimes think Allard Lowenstein is nothing but a dilettante playing at being a Congressman. A few months ago, he told me the most important thing going on in the district was the coalition's plans to put up low-income housing in Inwood. He offered to put all the facilities of his office at our disposal.

Ever since, I've been trying, without luck, to get in touch with him.

April 15

Three letters, all vicious, all inspired by the ad in the *Times*, all accusing me of anti-Semitism, and all sent by dissident members of my congregation, were read aloud at tonight's temple board meeting.

As equal time for me, Bob Mandel read his reply to each of the letters, in which he defended my right to speak as a private citizen. In two of the letters, the members resigned from the congregation, bringing to five the total number of resignations in the last month.

"Has either of those couples pledged to contribute to the building fund?" one of the more practical board members asked.

None had.

April 16

In my confirmation class this afternoon the kids arranged a debate between me and a geometry teacher at the high school who is a strict Protestant fundamentalist. He arrived with sixteen pages of scribbled notes and a Bible underlined with his own yellow, red, and blue markings.

"I am going to show you," he announced, flexing his Bible, "that we have only two alternatives: either Christ is God, or he is a phony."

There were giggles in the classroom.

"In the Old Testament, the Jews were God's chosen people," he began, citing the appropriate passages from the yellow markings in the Bible. "And we are told that God's chosen people would eventually announce the coming of the Messiah who was God incarnate." More appropriate passages, this time marked in blue. "And the New Testament clearly shows that Jesus was the promised Messiah." He pointed out where it said so in the passages set off with red.

After about a half hour of this, the kids were throwing me stares of excited anticipation. *Go on in there, Rabbi. Give him hell.* It felt odd having them on *my* side, for a change.

"I'm sure Jesus believed he was the Messiah," I said to him. "But I don't. I think we have to be a little more rational about these things."

The geometry teacher was clutching his Bible. "It says here Jesus was the Messiah," he said.

"Who cares what the Bible says?" I said. "That doesn't mean anything."

"Doesn't mean anything!" he shouted. "God wrote the Bible."

"Don't be ridiculous," I said. "God didn't write the Bible. God isn't capable of writing anything."

"Do you mean to tell me that as a rabbi you don't believe that God wrote the Bible?"

"Of course God didn't write the Bible."

"Then who did?"

"Men did," I said. "And men today are still writing the Bible. In fact, you and I are probably doing a draft of it right now."

"You don't seem to take it seriously," he said with contempt.

"I take it seriously," I said. "But not literally."

"You don't believe it?"

"It's not to be believed. It's to be read, and studied simply as a chronicle of man's view of himself. The Bible is a living, developing document."

"And you don't believe what happens in the Bible?" He wasn't listening.

"What *happens* in the Bible is not important," I said "Only what we learn from what is said to have happened is important. Today's Bible might be written from the headlines about the Vietnam war. Yet it's not the war itself which is important. It's the context in which it occurred and what else happened along with and because of it. That's what's important. Years from now man will have manufactured myths about Vietnam which will show only that at a particular time man had a particular view of himself. If the myths also give us a hint of what really happened, that is incidental."

"So you think the Bible is a fairy tale?" He was angry.

"Have you ever heard any story told a dozen times by a dozen different people come out the way it started? By the time the twelfth person is relating it, you know more about the eleven people before him than about the story itself. That's what happened with the Bible. That's why it's mythical. It may or may not have a determinable basis in fact, but if it does, there's not much of one.

"Every man operates on the basis of his self-myth, the way in which he views himself. People with similar self-myths tend to come together politically to fashion their society as an extension of their own view of themselves. Each society struggles with itself over which of its myths will prevail. For instance, in America, at this particular time, Nixon is operating on one myth and youth is operating on another. Nixon's myth is triumphant. Twenty years from now, it probably won't be. But forty years from now, the prevailing myth could be pseudo-Nixonian again. The Bible is simply a record of thousands and thousands of years of myths—myths like Nixon's, and myths like the kids', but myths, evolving, recurring, changing myths which tell us only about man's constant quest for a larger meaning of himself."

"Did we come here to talk politics or discuss the Bible?" the geometry teacher asked me. "What about *our* New Testament? I suppose you think that's all a myth, too?"

"Not all a myth," I said, "but a *collection* of myths. One part of it, the story of Jesus, is an attempt to personify the feeling of the turbulent times when the world was going through a convulsive culture conflict similar to what we are going through today. The story of Jesus was the controlling myth of that time—tranquility in the turbulence, like Nixon in America—and it eventually led to a new civilization which developed its own myths. With Jesus, or anywhere else in the Bible, one myth is the story, another is its interpretation, and they form an infinite number of combinations. Myth upon myth, the Bible can be interpreted and reinterpreted and then, and only then, can we find for ourselves our own ultimate myth of substance in our existence. The Bible is a 4,000-year collection of myths which reflect some meaning from which we can see that a civilizing process has been going on in the world."

"I suppose you think the Creation is a fairy tale, too?"

"Of course. It's a very silly story. Imagine, God creating this world in six days."

"Then how do you think the world was created?"

"Your guess is as good as mine. Every civilization has its own creation story. Among the things they have in common, however, is that they are usually grouped with a flood story. Did you ever wonder why? What is this all about? What does it mean? Well, to me, anyway, it means that something happened to man at the time the myths developed, the stories of which are an expression. Something happened to man's view of himself, to his understanding of himself.

"In the beginning, man obviously worshipped nature and animals, but then through his creation and flood myths, it becomes apparent that he began to believe in himself, in his own power to do things, to overcome things. Nature did its worst; a flood ravished the earth. And man *prevailed.* That's the point. For the first time man saw himself as the capstone of creation. This was a tremendous revolution in thought for him. But he knew he couldn't have done it himself. So he saw himself in covenant with God—something unknown and larger than himself—prevailing over animals and nature

"What happened is that man discovered religion, and viewed his own importance and significance through it. He could prevail over the environment because of a covenant with God, in which he was the junior partner. He lived believing in himself, but with a greater deference for that which is larger than himself. God became a dimension of man."

"And then God sent the Messiah to His people," the geometry teacher interjected.

"No," I said. "And then along came a man called Jesus Christ, and some people said that God so loved the world that he was giving them His only begotten son. To think in these terms, which Judaism has always resisted, is to make of God another man. Christianity makes the whole universe *human.* It teaches that man is no longer the junior, but the equal partner. It makes too much of man himself. There is no humility in this. Yet it so predominates our thinking these days, that now man is coming to regard himself not as the junior, not as equal, but as the *senior* partner in the covenant. Modern man has grown so sure of himself he no longer thinks of conceding what he doesn't know."

"And I suppose you think Jews are the only people who can believe in God anymore?"

"Of course not," I said. "Judaism never taught us to believe *in* God. You think I am saying that Jews are the only people who are truly religious. That's not true either. These days the one segment of society which tends to be most religious isn't even aware of religion. I am talking about the kids. They are really trying hard to relate to some greater whole: they call it love; they call it community; they express it through rock music. Rock music is probably today's Bible. Like Vietnam, or the new morality, rock music will become a recorded myth of our time. And like the ancient myths, they will collect in history until another generation finds its mythical substance through them. The Bible is the substance of the past, and its underlying reality is always and only man's existence in this universe."

"You call rock and roll the Bible! You defile the name of Christ!"

There was obviously no communication between the two of us. I suppose I was as guilty as he, because whatever he said that was not in direct reply to me was so meaningless I can't even remember it. Because he had come intending to proselytize, and I ended up doing most of the talking, he left the session very angry.

The kids? I think they enjoyed the exchange, although unfortunately not so much for what was in it, as for the spectacle it was.

April 21

This morning's newspaper carried a photograph of black students, armed with bandoliers and rifles, emerging from a building they had occupied at Cornell University. The blacks said they had the rifles because they felt threatened.

I believe them. A black student today is stripped of two very important defenses. First of all, he is brought directly from the ghetto to the campus, where he is without his only *real* base of support, his own community. Secondly, he is considered an object for extra-special help who is required to answer to lower-than-normal academic standards, and this removes his human psychological defense in the event he fails.

These two factors, with good reason, probably led to a collective nervous breakdown among the blacks at Cornell.

April 22

Today, in a regular class I conduct for the ladies of my congregation, I was asked why the Jewish people have survived.

I said that we have survived for any number of reasons, not the least of which is that we have considerable experience in surviving, which has given us a certain flexibility in dealing with threatening situations. We are also historically diversified, and therefore if any one of us or any group of us is in difficulty, there is another one of us or group of us prospering at the same time. A case in point here is the overwhelming financial and psychological support American Jewry gave the Israelis during the Six-Day War in 1967. Another possible reason for our survival is that Judaism has been a satisfying way of life to us, and generation after generation has worked to preserve it. Another is that our survival is a miracle, a matter of divine intervention to perpetuate the special role invested in us. All these things, or any combination of them, have a certain validity.

April 23

I was invited to attend a meeting tonight of the Five Towns Forum, a group founded in the McCarthy era by leftists who felt a need to hang together in the vicious onslaught. Its members are now in their forties and fifties, and despite their anti-Vietnam feelings, are very much out of touch with the New Left. As a result, there is a conscious effort to keep up.

For the last nine years the group has held an annual joint dinner with the NAACP, which, of course, nine years ago took a certain, minimal amount of courage. Tonight, on the grounds that the NAACP is no longer militant enough, they voted to discontinue that meeting. Instead, they have begun to make arrangements this year for a cocktail-party benefit for the Black Panthers.

I got a call this evening from the father-in-law of the girl who broke down and cried when I asked her to read Martin Buber as part of her preparation to convert to Judaism. He is anxious to get her converted.

"How long does it take to have a conversion, Rabbi?" the father-in-law asked me.

"I try to make each conversion a custom-made thing to suit the individual," I said.

"Well," he said, "why don't you custom-make this one to get it over with quickly? I don't like the girl living without a religion."

April 24

I received a copy today of a bulletin mailed out by the social action committee of Temple Israel. "Dear Friends," it began. "We have frequently discussed at our meetings the need in our community for a central committee composed of representatives of all the various organizations interested in local social problems. We believe, after previous unsuccessful attempts, the newly formed Five Towns Coalition is answering this need. The president of the coalition is Rabbi Martin Siegel, Temple Sinai, Lawrence. In his comparatively short residence here, Rabbi Siegel has made a strong impact both by his ability and dedication to principles for which the Jewish religion stands. We are very fortunate in having him as our guest at the next meeting of our committee which will be held on Tuesday, May 6."

I was touched. Really.

April 25

In a conciliatory mood last week, I called one of the men from the ADL who had come out to see me and told him I would like to hold a dialogue service in my congregation on the subject of blacks and Jews. I asked him to recommend somebody at the ADL with whom to hold the dialogue. He gave me a man's name, and I called him.

The man was very rude. "You'll have to come in and see me," he said. "We'll have to talk it over."

"Talk what over?"

"Well, we have to be sure how you're going to handle this thing," he said. "We have to be sure we're not going to be embarrassed."

"My God," I said. "It's going to take place in a synagogue!"

He said he didn't care; he wouldn't discuss the matter any further over the phone. I hung up on him.

Instead, I invited Mr. Harold Applebaum, regional director of the American Jewish Committee, a group which has maintained a more reasonable tone on the black anti-Semitism issue. The dialogue took place tonight, prompting a large turnout, which indicates the very strong feelings in the congregation on the subject.

I began the discussion by saying that both the Jews and the blacks are insecure—although for different reasons—and therefore have not been able to communicate because both feel oppressed, and also each, to an extent, sees the other as the oppressor. Many in the congregation were still reacting to the week's events at Cornell, where some of their children are students. One member said he had been to Cornell for Parents' Weekend and was shoved out of the student union building by a black militant. "Things have gone on long enough," this man said. "We have got to stop the blacks."

"I agree," another fellow said. "The only thing a bad child understands is a stick, and we have to discipline these children just as we would discipline our own children. This is the only way the colored kids are going to understand."

"We've been treating the blacks like children all along," I said. "Now they are no longer reacting obediently."

"Look," another member said. "I'm just an ordinary man living an ordinary life and I just can't worry about all these things—blacks, justice, truth. I'm simply trying to make a living and live a decent life. If the blacks bother me, what can I do? I'll just have to fight back to survive."

Despite a scattering of remarks like this, the congregation was surprisingly sympathetic to the blacks. Like Mr. Applebaum, they spoke primarily from the secular point of view, assessing the situation in terms of whites (not Jews) and blacks.

The interesting thing about the evening is that the issue of black anti-Semitism was never once mentioned. So pass the styles. As it becomes increasingly apparent that the New York State legislature will pass a compromise decentralization bill, Jews are finally coming to their senses. They now find that black anti-Semitism was more a myth than a peril. Jewish groups like the ADL are also growing ambivalent. Sensing that their role as spokesmen and defender of the Jewish people is threatened, the ADL is now indicating that it has *turned the corner* and is now working to *solve* the problem. They are in a very lovely position, of course: helping to create a problem, and then pronouncing it solved, and in the course of these events, perpetuating themselves.

April 27

It's been months, or at least weeks, since I've heard a word from my Congressman. The last time Lowenstein called, he said, "Rabbi, I have a picture of us together, and I was going to send it to you, but I'd rather give it to you in person so you'll know how much I appreciate your efforts."

I'll bet he says that to all his congregants—I mean constituents.

But I still haven't seen the picture.

Lowenstein comes to mind because this afternoon, at the traditional meal of consolation following a funeral I conducted, I happened to meet a close friend of Al's. I'd never met the man before, but we started talking, and I told him that having Al Lowenstein for your Congressman is like having no Congressman at all.

April 28

I got a call from Al Lowenstein at seven o'clock this morning. It was so early I don't even remember what he said.

I have to sympathize with Al's very blatant approach to quelling my dissatisfaction. I often do the same thing. Like a Congressman, a rabbi must have a reasonably good information network or he won't survive.

The name of the game is *preventive maintenance*. Somebody in the congregation has been sick, and he is piqued because I haven't called. Word gets to me. I call.

"How are you?" I say. "This is Rabbi Siegel. I understand you haven't been feeling well."

Small talk.

They know I know and I know they know that the only reason I'm calling is that somebody has told me they are angry that I didn't call. But all it is is a ritual dance and we all feel better afterward.

All day I didn't once feel antagonistic toward Lowenstein.

April 30

I found the students in my class at the Woodmere Academy relieved today, because the matter of Ivy League college admissions was over. They were eager to talk about what they called their "ultimate values," which to them seemed to mean getting married, being successful, and holding onto Judaism solely as an identification. They felt they occupied a privileged position and that it was therefore no responsibility of theirs to serve mankind or society or anything other than themselves. The session depressed me, because many of the students sounded like elitist snobs ready to go out and take whatever they can get from the world, and also because after an entire year as their teacher, I don't think I've moved them an inch.

To compound the depression, I later had to conduct a rehearsal, the second or third of its kind, for the confirmation services to be held in a few weeks. In many respects, the affair has turned into a big empty pageant—a march with flowers, and speeches, and the various trappings of pomp—so huge that we had to suspend classes for the month prior to the event just to rehearse. The parents expect the confirmation to look like a gala scene from the *Marriage of Figaro.*

After the rehearsal today, one of the more sensitive students asked to speak to me privately. He said he had a question about the sermon I gave on *Portnoy's Complaint* several weeks ago.

"What is it?" I asked.

"Well," he said, "I wasn't sure whether you said premarital sex was against the Jewish religion."

"I didn't say anything about it."

"Well," he said. "I'd like to know. Is it?"

"Judaism makes no big deal about sex," I said. "The Bible says a man should have sex with his wife, and the Ten Commandments say that a husband shouldn't have sex with any woman except his wife."

"Yes, but what if he doesn't have a wife?"

"It doesn't say."

"What's your opinion?" he asked.

"Personally I would like to see the importance of sex deflated. I don't think people should be so involved with whether to do it or not."

"I don't understand."

"Sex should be a part of an enduring relationship," I said. "It's only one form of emotional expression among many."

"Does this mean you have to be married to have sex?"

"No."

"Well," he said, "if you have sex and you're not married, does Judaism approve?"

"As far as I can see, it doesn't rule it out."

"Well, how can you tell if you're doing the right thing?"

"That's up to you. It should be a level of communication, not just an act of gratification."

"Then that means you don't have to be married to have sex?"

"That means sex doesn't have to be limited to marriage."

"Well," he asked. "How do you feel? Do you condone premarital sex?"

"I understand it."

After this conversation, I felt guilty about being so evasive, and if it were just I, Marty Siegel, talking, I would have answered him differently. But he wasn't asking Marty Siegel. He was asking the Rabbi. And as the Rabbi, I don't consider it my role to sanction or disapprove of whatever he is doing. I didn't think it was as important to answer his questions as it was to listen to them. Besides, if I had been more direct, his mother would have been calling me tonight accusing me of encouraging her son to sleep with his girl friend. I've been through it all before.

My own feelings toward sex are quite liberal, because I regard sex as a step toward a deepening relationship. And as I told the young man, I find that sex is communication, and therefore is religious in itself. If somebody is sexually inhibited, then by my definition, he is also religiously inhibited.

This is not to say that sex should be instant when man and woman meet each other, but rather that sex is appropriate when the relationship invites it. That usually means that there's a commitment of one sort or another between the partners, and for many people it does not take a state of marriage to have that commitment. Yet, for many, it does.

As a rabbi, I can't oppose premarital sex on moral grounds. That would be silly. Most couples sleep together before they marry, anyway, so they are not exactly going to bed on their wedding night with the sanctity of God. While I may refuse to come down from Mt. Sinai and shoot thunderbolts at these people, to be honest, something about many of them disturbs me. For these people, their sex life is an extension of their your "own thing" ethic. It's selfish. Commitments are to be avoided. They believe simply in doing whatever pleases them.

Sex, like marriage, implies the willingness to give something up, and only in that context can it be an element around which real relationship develops.

May 2

At this evening's service, the Torah portion dealt with the sanctity of the Sabbath, and I used the occasion to deliver a sermon on the declining significance of the Sabbath in our lives. In the past, people used the Sabbath as a day of prayer, rest, and contemplation, and through it gained a quality of relatedness with another. A day of reflection allowed them to put the affairs of their lives in perspective which today, because we are too busy to observe the Sabbath, we do not have. Judith took the sermon quite seriously. Otherwise, I don't think it had much of an effect

Practically nobody showed up to hear it.

May 3

Al Lowenstein called me again yesterday when I was out, and I didn't call him back. If he wants to talk to me, he can call me again. I've put in my share of unreturned calls to him.

The New York State legislature has acted on the school decentralization law, and in the last several days I've been on the phone a great deal discussing it. The general feeling seems to be that the issue has at least begun to resolve itself.

Under the new law, community school boards will be elected and will have the power to employ a district superintendent and establish his powers and duties. The local boards will be able to operate local community centers and recreational facilities, make minor repairs to their school buildings and submit proposals for remodeling and new construction.

Other than that, the concessions at best are halfway. The local boards will be empowered to hire and fire their own teachers, but they can't violate any of the current agreements between the Board of Education and the United Federation of Teachers. They will also be able to select their own textbooks and instructional materials, but these have to be approved by the chancellor—the new designation for the city's superintendent of schools.

If nothing else, the concept has triumphed.

May 4

With my swimming pool completed, I've been anxiously awaiting word from the executive committee of the temple on my contract renewal, but today I learned that at a meeting last week the members decided to put off for a few months any further discussion of my tenure. From what I understand, the general feeling was that they would like to retain me, but with summer approaching, they're not in the proper frame of mind for such serious business. I don't mind the wait; it only strengthens my bargaining position.

Today was such a sunny, exhilarating spring day that I spent most of it in the pool splashing around with little Sally. Judith watched for a few minutes, but said she didn't want to come in.

Later in the afternoon, I drove to the barber. On the way, I entered a narrow congested street where traffic was moving very slowly. The man in the car behind me began honking furiously and followed me closely until we reached a red light, where he jumped out of his car, rushed over to my window and screamed some really crude things at me. I ignored him, but when the light changed and I began to drive off, he spit at me.

Times like this really make me understand how protected I am in my position. People usually hold back in the presence of a rabbi. Maybe next year I'll ask the state to send me a license plate with *RABBI* spelled out on it to protect me from getting too many more insights into what life is really like.

May 5

The old-line planning and coordinating charity organization in the Five Towns is the Community Council, a group which is affiliated with the Community Chest and takes a very conservative approach in its efforts. Traditionally, the Council has had a virtual monopoly on coordinating doing good, but with the emergence of the Five Towns Coalition, they are beginning to fear their position is threatened.

The possibility of a conflict over which of us has the right to coordinate which good deeds is provoking some bitterness in the community. In light of this silliness, I asked the members of the executive committee of the coalition to be very conciliatory. Tonight I attended a meeting of the Community Council and pledged that we would never duplicate anything they are doing, and that when it was possible, we would work with them, except that we would not be influenced by the sometimes old-fashioned priorities generated by the Community Chest.

During the meeting, one lady, who serves as vice-chairman of the Community Chest and is Mrs. Charity Establishment of the Five Towns, interrupted me quite angrily. "Rabbi," she said, "did I understand you to say that the Community Chest does not do anything?"

"No, I didn't mean to imply that," I said.

"Well," she continued, unfazed, "if you had lived in this community a little longer, you would know what you are talking about."

'Madam," I answered her, "there are now new approaches to charity, just as there are innovations in many areas, and in order to undertake these innovations, we usually have to overcome the obstacle of ignorance of which you are a very fine example."

After the meeting, feeling that I was a bit too strong, and

in an effort to avert a civil war of charity, I took the lady aside and told her that I would like to get to know her better and break down some of our differences of opinion.

"You, Rabbi," she said, "are an arrogant and rude young man."

"Well, I'm glad to finally meet a woman who knows everything." I walked away.

The lady is one of the few Roman Catholics active in community affairs, and that fact certainly contributed to our confrontation. She didn't like the idea of being challenged by a young upstart Jew.

May 6

Tonight, after a meeting of the social action committee of Temple Israel, one of the members said to me, "Rabbi, there's something I've been meaning to tell you for a long time."

"What's that?" I said.

"You remind me very much of Congressman Lowenstein."

May 7

We held another rehearsal today for the confirmation pageant, and it bored me so much I canceled next week's rehearsal.

Two of the long-haired members of the class came up to me

afterward and announced they did not want to be confirmed. "I don't believe in Judaism," one said.

"You don't have to," I said. "If you participate in the Jewish community, you are a Jew. You can believe anything you want."

He seemed satisfied, and consented to go through with his confirmation. The other said he didn't want to be confirmed if it were just part of a theatrical production, which he thought it was. I secretly admired him. I wouldn't want to be confirmed under these circumstances, either.

May 8

The school board election was held yesterday, and Jim Deleston, the black candidate I supported, received only 600 votes. He lost to a white candidate who got 3,200 votes.

May 10

I conducted a wedding today for a doctor I'd known in the Marine Corps. I hadn't seen him in five years, and he touched off memories of my brief military career.

I never intended to join the Marines. When I graduated from Hebrew Union, with an obligation to serve as a chaplain for two years in some branch of the military, I opted for the Navy. Why not? I look good in blue, I like ships and I still had that college feeling of wanting to be accepted in an Anglo-Saxon milieu.

Nobody told me the Marines were part of the Navy. But after I completed Navy chaplain school, I found out. I received my orders, shipping me to Camp LeJeune, North Carolina, the home of 60,000 Marines, only 150 of whom were Jewish.

The base was situated outside Jacksonville, North Carolina, one of those horrible Southern towns that feeds off the local military. One day, I was invited to a cocktail party at an elegant mansion, and after a long conversation with the host, I realized that he'd made no reference to his occupation; that's usually the first thing people mention, over cocktails. Finally, I asked him what he did for a living. He told me that, among other things, he ran the town tattoo parlor.

That was the kind of place Jacksonville was. The town's elite ran tattoo parlors, movie theaters, and credit jewelry shops. Everything was outrageously priced, but available, of course, on "convenient credit terms." I waged a steady war against the local merchants, many of whom were Jewish. One of them once called me in the middle of the night. "Keep out of our business affairs," he said, "or I'm going to arrange to have you killed."

I survived, quite comfortably. I had three secretaries, a driver and plush offices. I felt more like the vice-president of some great corporation than a rabbi.

I didn't spend much time pontificating about God. The men had practical, not spiritual problems—the sergeant hated them; their girl friend was pregnant; they were in debt—and I provided practical services. Once I imported lox and bagels for a Sunday breakfast.

No one ever accused me of being a model Marine. I didn't like to salute, and I talked to a private the same way I talked to a general—and vice-versa. I got away with this, of course, because I was the base's only Jewish chaplain, and no officer would dare reveal himself to be anti-Semitic.

Still, I was part of the military, and, whether I liked it or not, I had to contend with certain elements of military bureaucracy—fitness reports, for instance. The colonel who made out the report on me was an authoritarian nut. Once he had signs put up all over the base which read: DON'T WALK ON THE GRASS.

I walked on the grass, anyway.

The colonel spotted me. "Chaplain," he said, "can't you read?"

"Yes, Colonel," I said. "But I think I should advise you that it's not the colonel's grass I'm walking on. It's God's grass. And since I am God's local representative, I have the right to walk on it."

That was one bad fitness report.

The colonel lived by his own Golden Rule: Do unto others anything that will help you become a general. I'm afraid I didn't always advance his chances for promotion. Once, he was put in command of a large maneuver, a mock invasion of a place called Hilton Head Island, a resort center; our invasion was to commemorate the founding of the island. The colonel put me in charge of civilian liaison. I promptly arranged with the chef at a local hotel to provide hors d'oeuvres for a celebration when we landed. After all, I was Jewish first, a Marine second.

I was so busy making the catering arrangements that, when the invasion began, I missed the ship. The colonel was furious; he dreaded having to report to his superior that, on his dry run at playing general, one of his men was missing. He called me over the ship-to-shore radio. "Chaplain," he bellowed, "how are you prepared to get back to the ship?"

"Colonel," I said, "I'm going to walk on the water."

Several days later, after somebody explained my little joke to him, the colonel threatened me with another bad fitness report. "Sir," I said, "the worst you can do with your fitness report is roll it up in a little ball and throw it at me."

I was quickly transferred out of his battalion.

Most chaplains were not that frivolous about their fitness reports. Many of them joined the military as a career, and they knew that one poor fitness report could cost them a promotion. They looked upon themselves as officers before clergymen, and, inevitably, they took an overly cautious approach to everything they did. Often, non-Jewish Marines came to me for aid, because their own chaplain, a career man, would not take the risks involved in helping them.

The military, by its very nature, demanded an antiseptic approach to religion. Morality was rigidly prescribed, and theology limited to an acceptable general pattern calculated to offend no one. Even though the chaplaincy appears to be the military's one concession to the fact that it deals with human beings—not automatons—the military still seemed to me to use religion only to justify its larger purposes.

The only way to improve this situation is to remove the chaplaincy completely from the military and bring it under civilian control. Then clergymen will be clergymen, not majors-who-want-to-be-colonels, and religion will have a chance to be religion, not just another facet of the military code of behavior.

May 13

The youth rebellion is seeping down. Recently, the seventh and eighth-graders confronted our religious-school administration with demands that they help shape the curriculum. They said they also wanted an improved teaching staff. At present, many of our faculty members are public-school teachers and they teach Judaism as if it were arithmetic. The kids also asked for more community-type activities, such as camping trips.

This evening I presented their proposed reforms and my own to the temple's board. The immediate reaction was, "We can't afford anything that's going to cost us money. We are putting up a new building and we have to be careful not to overspend in other areas."

I argued for two hours that what goes into the building is more important than the building itself. Eventually, their resistance broke down. By 11:30 they approved all the reforms we asked for.

We are now going to restructure the curriculum away from traditional subjects like history and concern ourselves more with concepts. The year will be divided into a series of six-week segments in each of which we will hold intensive seminars on a theme.

In the first six-week segment, for instance, we will discuss the concepts of justice and mercy, tracing them through the Biblical tradition, the Hebrew tradition and into modern times. The students will not only debate whether Cain was justified in killing Abel, but whether the Israelis were justified in executing Eichmann.

Each six-week segment will begin with an all-day session and will conclude with a discussion between students and their parents. Also, in addition to the seminars, the students will have brunches and trips and singing sessions to encourage them to develop a sense of community among themselves.

May 15

"That was a great sermon you gave last week," somebody told me today.

I appreciated the compliment, except for one thing: I can't remember the sermon.

May 16

At services tonight, I delivered a sermon on the state of the Jewish religion. I recalled how in the last generation the obsessive issue among the Jewish people was what kind of a Jew one was going to be—Orthodox, Conservative or Reform—and how the decision probably had as much to do with the socio-economic status (the more assimilated, the more affluent, the more *reformed*) as it did with principle. Practically nobody had any doubt about remaining Jewish, so only the little differences became the big issues: people quibbled over whether to wear a hat or not to wear a hat; whether to use a *tallith* or not to use a *tallith;* whether to celebrate Rosh Hashanah on one day or two days. Only the externals were a matter of concern, only the rites; everybody remained positively Jewish.

The current generation faces a more serious question: whether or not to be Jewish at all. The Orthodox, Conservative and Reform movements have all lost touch with their followings. Unconcerned, they seem to be moving toward a middle ground, with Reform coming back to tradition, and Orthodox and Conservative finally yielding to some modern influences. But, meanwhile, more and more young Jews will have nothing to do with any Jewish movement.

The hope—if there is any at all within the framework of formal religion—is in real *reformed,* not Reform, Judaism. Reform Judaism today carries too much dead weight, people who are seeking an easy Judaism, fitted to convenience, which they often use as an excuse to simply worship themselves as the center of value. The *reformed* Judaism that I am trying to implant at Temple Sinai is *innovative* Judaism. I see this as religion with a creative potential in which each individual is allowed creative release. Unlike Reform Judaism, which for many people requires only a guilty conscience, *reformed* Judaism demands knowledge, commitment and a willingness to experiment.

At a service several months ago, I noticed an interesting-looking girl sitting in the congregation. I didn't know her name. In the traditional greeting line after the service, I said to her, "Hello, I'm Rabbi Siegel. I don't believe I know your name."

She got furious. "We met before," she said. "And if you ask me my name one more time, I won't ever come back to services."

After services tonight, I saw her again, and having forgotten the whole previous incident, I walked up to her and said, "Hello, I'm Rabbi Siegel. I don't believe I know your name."

That was the end of her formal Judaism.

May 18

At religious school this morning, the students seemed anxious to talk to me about their teachers. They said that they were most comfortable in classes where the teacher listened to them as well as taught them. I agree with them, and have already made plans to fire two of the faculty members because they have neither the flexibility nor the intelligence required to listen.

A man who is a supervisor in the New York City public schools came to see me today and asked for my views on the teachers' strike. I told him I supported community control. He said he agreed with me—and asked if I would conduct the unveiling service for his mother's tombstone. He explained that he needed a rabbi with the correct point of view.

The man—who is not a member of my congregation—put me in a very difficult position: I am, by profession, a servant to all Jews, but I am also paid and supported by one particular congregation of Jews. If I agreed to do everything every Jew requested of me—on ceremonial occasions, the demand for rabbis seems to far exceed the supply—I would be neglecting the people I'm hired to serve.

I've never learned how to draw the line.

I agreed to conduct the unveiling service.

May 20

As I was leaving the house tonight to attend a meeting where I was to be inducted as a member of the board of the Nassau County Girl Scouts, Judith said to me, "Martin, you know sometimes I feel like I have to make an appointment to see you."

"What do you mean?" I asked.

"Just that," she said. "You seem to be so involved with other things you don't have any time left for Sally and me anymore."

"Judith, that's not true," I said. "Sally and you have always come first. Above everything else."

"Well, I think you're just not available anymore."

I didn't argue any further with her. Judith is not a very verbal person, and I sensed she was probably talking around a larger problem she's facing, although I'm not sure what it is. I decided not to go to the meeting, and we spent the night discussing how I would try to give more time to my family.

Later, I went for a walk by myself and passed a neighbor of ours, a doctor, getting into his car.

"Rabbi," he said. "How are you feeling? Judith told me you haven't been too well."

I know that was meant to be a signal from Judith.

Something is wrong.

PART TWO

May 21

Judith is behaving very strangely. She spent part of the day doing her housework, but more slowly, more deliberately than she usually does, as if she were separated from what she was doing. I'm concerned about her.

For a few hours this afternoon, we sat in silence by the pool. She didn't want to talk. Whatever was happening within her mind she wouldn't share with me. Maybe she couldn't. I don't know. We were both in our bathing suits, and after a while, I dove into the water.

"Come on, dear," I called to her, playfully. "Come on in." She has not been swimming since the pool was completed.

"Martin, please," she said. That was *all* she said.

Tonight Judith remained at home when I went to the temple to participate in the consecration service which annually precedes the confirmation pageant.

The students were in a springlike mood, and they romped through the service in an unusually carefree manner. Some of them were lighthearted to the point of being silly, and the service was interrupted several times by laughter and applause.

Afterward, I was confronted by a delegation of older congregants. "How could you allow this to go on?" they asked. "How can you allow applause and laughter in the synagogue, the House of God?"

"Because it's a place where we all should have tears *and* joy," I said. "It's a place where we should all be ourselves, not simply carbon copies of piety."

I didn't argue any further. I left. There were other things on my mind.

May 22

Today I conducted a burial service for the funeral of Robert Goodman, a sensitive and kind man, the father of Andrew Goodman, the young civil-rights worker who was slain with two friends in Mississippi in the summer of 1964. Goodman, who was only fifty-four years old, was a civil engineer who wrote poetry. He never psychologically recovered from his son's murder.

The funeral took place at Manhattan's Community Church, probably because it was the largest place available to accommodate the nearly 2,000 people who attended. A total of five people gave eulogies, one of Goodman's friends read from T. S. Eliot, a Bach fugue was played, and the casket was rolled out. I felt a little uncomfortable with the situation: *everything was too good, too perfect, too controlled.*

Although there were tears throughout the events, there was, quite distinctly on the part of those crying, no hope, no divine dimension, no relationship to anything other than this lovely man who was now dead. These were good and kind people, almost all of them very intelligent, yet they had no overreaching context in which they lived. They had no feeling for anything other than the immediate.

They said to me and to one another that Robert Goodman would live on in their memories—a decent gesture, but one in which they were making too much of themselves. That was their problem. They saw themselves as the source of all value, because the values they chose to follow they themselves created and then believed in. They never rose to any greater dimension than themselves. They were prisoners in the moment of their own lives.

I rode out to the cemetery with two close friends of the family who had arranged the funeral, and had asked me, because of my reputation as a social activist, to officiate at the burial.

Because it was composed largely of family and close friends, the crowd at the cemetery was much more Jewish than it was at the church. Robert Goodman was buried next to his son's grave, which was marked with a rather large headstone on which a symbol of clasped hands had been engraved.

I met the two surviving Goodman sons. One wore his hair very long and had it pulled together in the back with a barrette. The other son, who had a beard and moustache, was a college student.

When I asked each of the sons to say Kaddish for their father, they refused. I explained to them that Kaddish was a prayer praising God for life. They both replied coldly that they had no connection with religion, and especially no connection with Judaism.

I said the Kaddish.

Afterward, I tried to get into a conversation with the son who is the college student, but because I represented Judaism, he was very antagonistic toward me. He didn't seem to want any communication.

As I was leaving the cemetery, I heard two women talking. "How did you like the funeral?" one asked the other. As if it were a play, and Clive Barnes would be writing the review in the next edition of the *Times*.

When I arrived home late in the afternoon Judith was sitting on the sofa in the living room, doing nothing. Just sitting.

May 23

It was the day of the pageant of confirmation, and, as expected, the show was a sellout—a glorious scene of gowns and flowers and all the other vestiges of pomp which draw the congregation to this annual rite of child worship. As well as reading the official prayers for the occasion, the kids wrote part of the service themselves, and gave short talks and various interpretations of the prayers. Then, in its high moment, the service concluded with what I call the Jewish Pledge of Allegiance: "I pledge myself to my people and to my people's faith. May I never do anything which will bring disfavor to my people, my family, or my God."

Amen.

Judith stayed at home, and I was anxious to get back to her, and therefore had to miss the round of parties following the pageant. There are usually between twenty and twenty-five of these parties, because each confirmee has his own. Last year by the time I had reached number fifteen, I was numb. I remember parking my car, walking up to the door, and suddenly being struck by an odd sensation: *I've been here before. Maybe not this street; maybe not this house; maybe not these people; but I've been here before.*

And then it all began to come back to me. This was the home of a former girl friend of mine. I dated her, and dozens like her, in my teens. My friends in Brooklyn would call her a JAP, or Jewish American Princess. We all made our pilgrimages to the Five Towns to see what the rich Jewish girls were like.

I remembered the old dating ritual. When I walked in the door, the girl's father would be sitting in the living room, puffing on his pipe, and he would look at me very suspiciously. I could never understand why. I felt he should be grateful. I was a nice Jewish boy coming to take out his daughter. And then the mother would come in from the kitchen. She was always solicitous. She'd want to know everything about me. Where I went to school. What my favorite subjects were. Where I intended to go to college. If I planned to be a doctor or a lawyer. Meanwhile, my date would still be upstairs getting into her beautiful dress.

She was *always* late.

May 25

"Martin," Judith said to me this afternoon. "Did you really mean what you said about Sally?"

"What, honey?"

"What you said about Sally getting out of control and me not being able to assert myself with her?"

Until recently, our daughter Sally was a helpless infant, but now, as she approaches the age of two, she is emerging into a personality of her own—a very strong personality. In her innocent exuberance, she rampages through the house and, with seemingly endless energy, shouts, screams, and tears things apart. She is a source of constant activity; rarely a moment passes which she does not dominate. Judith has not been able to control her.

"What I said to you, Judith," I answered her, "is that we have to be aware that Sally is a person now, and we have to treat her like one."

Unfortunately I had said more. I had told Judith not to

overwhelm the child with negative demands, like "Don't do this, Sally," and "Don't do that, Sally." It's not that I want Sally to have free rein, I told her, but I do think the most we should impose on her are a few broad outer limits within which she can develop her behavior according to her own instincts. She is a very bright child, and Judith has been treating her rigidly, instead of creatively.

I became concerned enough a few weeks ago to ask Judith to use more psychology on the child, not simply to insist she cannot do certain things, but to stay flexible, to outthink her, to create situations in which Sally herself can decide the manner in which she will or will not do things.

"Dear," I told Judith this afternoon, "we have to give Sally an opportunity to be herself. All we should do is set up a larger context in which she can operate. This requires a lot of patience from both of us."

"And you don't think I can handle her this way?" she asked, obviously feeling hurt.

"Of course you can," I said.

We talked it out and, as I spoke to her endearingly, for the first time in days she seemed to respond. Later in the afternoon, as we were sitting by the pool she said, "I think I understand. I feel better."

"Come on, let's go for a swim," I said.

"You go," she said. "I don't want to."

May 26

I wanted to give Judith a break from Sally, so last night the two of us went into New York and spent the night at the Plaza Hotel. We walked around the city this morning, window-shopping and watching the people. Later we rested and had dinner. Judith said she felt much better.

In the evening, we attended a meeting of the Committee for Local Democracy, an organization of way-out long-haired leftists from Brooklyn who advocate a return to Jeffersonian principles. Although I sympathize with some of their ideas, their style is overbearing. They act like they know everything. They take a very condescending attitude to those who are not in direct agreement with them. Sometimes it seems that their main purpose in existing is to admire their own minds.

In the course of the meeting, Judith grew very upset. "You are not really doing anything but a lot of talking," she told them, interrupting the meeting. "You really don't understand what's going on. You have no practical knowledge of the situation. You just think you know it all."

I was startled. Judith is a very shy, timid person who never speaks out in public. Her shrill, emotional, accusatory denunciation of this group is probably the single most uncharacteristic thing I have seen her do in the seven and a half years of our marriage. She was not herself, and worse yet, I don't think she knows who she is anymore.

There is something deeply troubling her, something going on inside her mind, something working at her sense of equanimity. At one moment, she is brooding, at another she is instantly excitable.

Tonight, after her outburst, we left the meeting.

May 27

Today was my thirty-sixth birthday, and in the mail were only two congratulatory messages, one from a merchant in Wheeling and another signed "The Congregation." I guess institutions don't get birthday cards.

The day was not pleasant. Judith and I celebrated it with dinner at a restaurant with my mother. It was a mistake for me at this time to allow the two of them to get together.

Judith has never known the phenomenon of the Jewish mother. Her own mother is a convert to Judaism who lives like a Christian aristocrat. Aloof and with an austere nature, she administers a household of servants in the family mansion in Charleston, South Carolina. As a mother, she is not very warm, and she has great difficulty expressing her real feelings. She encourages family relations to remain on a somewhat formal level. She has always tended to be emotionally uninvolved with Judith. On the other hand, my mother is the archetype Jewish mother, overbearing, aggressive and relentless in her affection. There is nothing *formal* about her. She is a lady who married her husband and fell in love with her son. To this day, she enjoys looking after some of the finer details of my life.

Judith was weaned on the virtues of tactfulness, but my mother never found tact a virtue. *You want something, you say so* is her philosophy, and nobody is spared from what she has to say. The unfortunate thing is that while I can deal with her criticism, Judith cannot. Judith's own mother would never criticize her so directly: Judith lacks the conditioning to cope with my mother's style. "You shouldn't allow her to bother you," I've told Judith time and again. "Just ignore her. She means well." But Judith is too sensitive to ignore her.

I never really understood what was going on between Judith and my mother until we moved to Woodmere. In Wheeling, we would see her only occasionally and if there was any tension between the two of them then, it was nothing more than the natural intramural rivalry anyone could expect.

But when we moved here, and we were less than an hour from my mother, things began to get out of hand. It has put me in a very difficult position. On the one hand, I don't want to hurt my mother, because I know that what she does is only the result of excessive love. On the other hand, Judith is meek, and she needs to feel my strength on her side. What I usually end up doing is criticizing my mother for Judith and then tactfully instructing my mother to handle things a little more mildly. But my mother has no experience with tact.

So tonight, in the course of dinner, my mother made a few of her typically blunt remarks—about housekeeping and child-raising—and Judith, more sensitive than ever, was near tears. Afterward, my mother was supposed to spend the night at our house, but I vetoed the idea and drove her home to Brooklyn.

May 28

Along with the other unpleasant events of this week, I had to fire three of our religious-school teachers. I told two of them face-to-face that the reason we had to let them go is that we are changing the structure of the school and that will require particular teaching skills which I did not think they possessed. I couldn't get the courage to face the third teacher. I sent him a letter.

This evening we had a meeting of the parents of the sixth- and seventh-graders in the religious school, in which I outlined the new program I intend to put into effect. Its purpose is to relate the Jewish tradition to the present. The major concern will no longer be only a matter of Jewish identity, but a matter of developing some real substance to that identity. The emphasis will be on community. I have replaced the teachers I fired with student rabbis; I feel they will provide the expertise and commitment needed to make it all work. I think this new approach is vital to the survival of a relevant congregation.

May 30

Judith didn't attend services tonight. I was rushing out of the synagogue to get home to her when the cantor stopped me. He said he had something very important to tell me, but wanted to speak confidentially. He brought me into a private room and closed the door. I couldn't imagine what was happening.

He looked me sternly in the eye. "Martin," he said, "when you talk to them about a new contract, ask for a lot of money."

"Huh?"

"The president told me that they had a lot of trouble getting a rabbi before they found you last time. You be sure and ask for a lot of money."

May 31

A lady, one of my disciples in the congregation, asked me today if I thought I were a prophet. The question really intrigued me, and although I didn't have any immediate answer I've been thinking about it all day long.

I've always been a loner. I'm not at any university or connected with any formal movement, and therefore I've never had a barometer on my brain. I don't know if other people share my thoughts.

I think that I sometimes have a kind of emotion which, to my understanding, would be associated with prophecy. It is a feeling I get when there are certain things I say. I feel at times that what I'm saying is more than me saying it, that the thoughts in the words are almost unconsciously compulsive. At these times, it's never a question of whether it's right or wrong, appropriate or inappropriate, I just say what I have to say, and I don't seem to have much control over it. This doesn't happen often, but sometimes it does.

If what I say at these times can—and I really doubt it will—have any real impact, then I am a prophet. But no man can call himself a prophet, and few prophets are recognized in their lifetime.

On the other hand, what the lady might have detected was a prophetic style.

I do have that.

When I came home for dinner tonight, Judith was nowhere in sight. She is usually either in the kitchen or the living room.

"Judith," I called. "Are you here? Where are you?"

This went on for two or three minutes.

"Judith, where are you?"

Still no answer.

A few minutes later, I found her sitting on the bed in our room, with the door open.

"Why didn't you answer me, dear?"

"I don't know," she said.

"What's for dinner?"

"Nothing."

June 1

Judith cried hysterically all through the night. I don't think she got any sleep. "What's the matter, dear?" I kept asking her. "Try and tell me what's the matter."

She couldn't.

"Martin, I just can't control myself," was all she could say. "Please help me."

Then she would cry again.

At nine o'clock this morning, I took her to a psychiatrist, and he put her on some sedatives. She has quieted a little, but she is still tense. She is exhausted, but fidgety. She is practically not functioning at all.

Judith has finally fallen asleep, and I am in my study, forcing myself to accept a realization I have been evading all week: my wife is having some sort of nervous breakdown.

But why?

I've been sitting for the past two hours tormenting myself with that question. Why? Is it my fault? Is it because I've neglected her? Is it because of what I said to her about raising Sally? I feel so guilty, but yet I know it's got to be more than just those things. I think. I don't know.

I'm really very confused.

I've tried reconstructing our entire relationship. I remember when we met. I was a rabbinical student and she was an undergraduate at the University of Cincinnati. There was some sort of meeting, a Zionist group, and she attended. I immediately noticed her, because she handled herself so differently from the other girls. She had a definite quality, a certain dignity that the others lacked. We began to talk and right off I found her to be a very special person. She was almost otherworldly, antique; she had a delicacy, a graciousness, a quietness. She almost seemed out of place in modern life. She was unique. She had this Old World aura about her. She had this genuine feeling for other people. She was so sensitive. So unself-concerned.

We began dating. At the time, I was in a miserable state of mind. I hated the dormitory, I hated my classes at Hebrew Union and I was lonely. Judith was what I wanted, what I needed. We became engaged.

She returned to South Carolina that summer, and on one weekend she flew up to New York with her parents. They came to meet my parents. But then, suddenly, in the course of that weekend, out of nowhere, Judith said, "Martin, I can't go through with it." I was hurt. I was confused. I couldn't understand.

Shortly after she went back to South Carolina, I learned she was in the hospital, recovering from an emotional breakdown.

A lot of time passed, six months or so—I heard she recovered—and I graduated from Hebrew Union and was ordained as a rabbi. The next thing I knew, I was in North Carolina with the Marines. She heard I was there and wrote me on the High Holy Days wishing me a Happy New Year. I wrote back. A few weeks later, we rekindled things, and we were married the following November.

That was seven and a half years ago.

Shortly after we were married, Judith had another breakdown, but it was not quite so serious as the first, and mostly residual. I had no doubts about marrying her, because I felt, perhaps naïvely, that love would take care of any emotional problems she had. I felt that she had never known in her home the kind of love I would teach her in ours.

And for all these years, everything worked perfectly fine. She grew much stronger, much more capable of coping with things than she was in the first few years of our marriage. She saw—she had to see—how much I needed her, how much I was emotionally dependent on her.

But now this breakdown. How can I understand it? After Judith has devoted practically every minute of her life to me, whom can I blame but myself?

June 2

A few weeks ago, when she was still well, Judith told me about a woman she had met who had a child of Sally's age. The two became involved in a discussion on the problems of motherhood. "I didn't tell her what you did for a living," she said to me. "And when she asked, it was too late. We were already friends."

She protested that she is not recognized for herself, but for the fact that she is my wife. The Rabbi's Wife. The role denies her any identity of her own.

"I'm tired of just being the rabbi's wife," she said at that time. "I want to be Judith. I want to be Mrs. Siegel."

June 3

I spent the day at home with Judith, feeding her heavy sedatives. We couldn't communicate. I fear she is getting worse.

In the evening she fell asleep early, and I was able to get to a meeting of the Five Towns Coalition. We discussed a proposal I had made several weeks back for a code of personnel practices to protect the rights of the domestic help in the community.

One woman, a social type who is an officer of the coalition, warned that such a code would be extremely controversial and would undermine the group's efforts in other areas. "Raising the price of maids could finish us as an effective social-action organization in this community," she said. At least, that's the way I heard it.

June 4

I received a call tonight from an officer of the congregation who told me that a member of the worship committee is very angry with me because I decided to make a few minor innovations in the format of the service without consulting him. "Rabbi Siegel wants to do everything his own way," he told this officer. "He doesn't want to listen to anybody."

An otherwise pleasant man, my critic is an autocrat in his official capacity. He has frequently scolded me for infractions of pulpit protocol. How could I allow a woman in a miniskirt on the pulpit? How could I allow a confirmation student to make a joke in the House of God? How could I allow people to applaud during services?

He represents the people in the congregation who are wedded to the old forms and who often thwart my efforts to update the service. Even though the service now has little meaning to younger congregants who would like to see a less stringent mode of worship, the old-liners stand adamantly for tradition. Today nudes may cavort all over the stage and screen, but for the worship committee, it is still a momentous issue to change "thou" to "you," which, incidentally, is one of my minor innovations my critics oppose.

What complicates the situation, I must admit, is the fact that the old-liners are the ones who actually attend the services. To modernize our style of worship might destroy the small constituency we now have, and yet not to would mean to further alienate the alienated.

June 5

Judith is showing a slight improvement, although she is still heavily dependent on tranquilizers. Today, for the first time all week, she did some housecleaning—not much, but some—which may be a small sign that she is once again beginning to function.

She has seen her psychiatrist a few times. Hopefully, he is helping her, but these things are so hard to measure. Her state of mind fluctuates erratically. The periods of normality are occasional, and her frequent lapses into gloom and despair indicate the problem is far from solved.

Having spent so much time at home in the last few weeks has made me realize how little time I had spent here in the months preceding Judith's breakdown. Except for meals, and an hour after lunch when I would rest, read, and play with Sally, I worked practically every morning, afternoon, and evening. (Even though some of these times I was in my study, I could have been a thousand miles away.) The only time Judith and I had together for ourselves was during meals, but recently Sally began eating with us and dominating every conversation. Until a few months ago, Judith would wait up for me to come home at night, but as she grew more and more fatigued from taking care of Sally all day, she began going to sleep before I got home.

So in recent months there has been little opportunity for any real communication between us. In the little time we had to talk, most of what we said dealt with the affairs of the household.

Until now, I don't think I really understood what Judith has been going through—how many things she had to do in a single day. Not only was there Sally to take care of, easily a full-time proposition in itself, but also this fifteen-room house, cooking, managing the family finances, shopping and catering to my personal needs. And she never had a diversion. She has no personal friends, no outside activities.

I only made things more difficult for her. I can see that now. To begin with, we have opposite natures: I am chaotic; she is fastidious. Although in one respect I think this was a source of strength to her—just keeping me in order gave her a sense of being needed—it was also probably a cause of much of her anxiety. In recent months, as I became more and more involved in various causes and organizations, I found myself doing such things as hopping a train to New York in the middle of the day without ever telling her, or anyone, where I was going. She would call the office, and the secretaries would tell her that I'd been out all afternoon and that they didn't know where I'd gone. She would worry. We also had some arguments about money. Although she is meticulous in managing it, I guess I'm a little careless about spending it. I have a habit of writing checks and then forgetting I wrote them, and she had to spend long evenings trying to balance the checkbook.

The first signals of her illness grew out of this conflict of our natures, and I missed them She had always made it her role to keep me organized, to remind me of appointments, to serve virtually as a walking catalogue of my commitments; I am constantly losing things—my glasses, my car keys, my papers—but she would always know where everything was. Then, a few weeks ago, she began forgetting to remind me about an appointment, and she no longer knew where my glasses were when I asked. She was overwhelmed. And this only upset her more. She knew I needed her, and she couldn't fulfill my needs.

I became more involved with my outside affairs, more remote from her. She became literally overrun with managing Sally, the house and me. And this, the doctor thinks, is where it all began. Her sense of order, her sense of serving me, her sense of being needed grew into anxieties. She worried so much about functioning well at all these levels that, ultimately, she couldn't function at all.

If she will only recover—oh God, please help her—if she will only return to normal, I won't let it happen again.

June 6

Since Judith's illness, I have been running the household. My in-laws, the Tobiases, arrived from Charleston today to help me out. Perhaps now I'll be able to get back to some of the work which has been piling up.

June 7

I conducted a bar mitzvah this morning. At the reception afterward, one of the bar mitzvah boy's relatives, a Conservative rabbi, became upset because bacon was served with the hors d'oeuvres.

"What kind of *shul* is this?" he complained to me.

"We're very broad-minded," I said. "We allow the caterer a free hand."

After a brief conversation with him, in which he also inveighed against Sabbath travel, I quietly left for the airport and flew to Wheeling to conduct a wedding for a young man I'd known there. Judith went with me.

We arrived at five o'clock and the wedding was underway at six. It was an interfaith ceremony, and I co-officiated with a priest whose church was ten blocks from my former congregation.

"Oh, Rabbi," the priest said to me, "I haven't seen you in a little while. How's everything down at the temple?"

My departure must have had a great impact on the community.

June 8

We arrived back in Woodmere this afternoon. Judith seemed a little better in Wheeling, and today she was even more improved. The Tobiases think she is recovering, that the breakdown was not a serious one.

In the early evening, I attended a cocktail party given by the Marriage Band, a social group within the congregation. Even though a number of these people are aware that Judith is having some difficulties, not a single person asked me how she was. The prevailing attitude in this community is not to meddle in other people's affairs. Everybody has his own little problems, and each keeps his to himself.

Since Judith's illness, I have become sensitive to the fact that neither of us has any close friends—only official acquaintances. This has made the events of the last several weeks more sad, more lonely and, I think, probably has injured Judith even further. A little kindness, a little warmth from anybody—if anybody would bother to take the trouble—would certainly go a long way toward helping her to recover. And yet she has not had the courtesy of even a single telephone call from anyone.

June 11

In the last several days, with only occasional relapses, Judith has been taking on more and more of her old responsibilities. She is, of course, very fragile, and I am watching to see that the burden does not become too great and, at the same time, trying not to damage her confidence to function again. Her parents are still here, and are providing extra support for her, too.

Both her parents, and especially her mother, are very formidable people, intelligent, controlled, and aloof. Having seen Judith through her previous breakdown, neither thinks that what she is going through now is very serious. Judith has always been very emotionally dependent on her mother, and in the last several days the two have spent a great deal of time together talking things out. I have a feeling that her mother has been a great help in bringing Judith out of this. Mrs. Tobias is a very strong individual. In Charleston, where she and her husband recently retired from a successful public-relations business, many of her friends characterize her as "a woman who thinks like a man."

Judith and I were supposed to go to a dinner tonight sponsored by the American Jewish Committee, the semi-elite of the Jewish secular organizations, but I didn't think she was well enough yet. I went alone. The purpose of the dinner was to award plaques for various achievements to various people. One of the rituals is to honor a Non-Jew of the Year. This year's Non-Jew of the Year (the title is mine; they call it something like a Brotherhood Award) went to a black who works in the poverty program on Long Island. It struck me that this was such a frivolous exercise. The blacks need our real help, and the Jewish organizations seem primarily concerned with giving them plaques.

The guest speaker was Rabbi Mark Tannenbaum, the director of the Interfaith Department of the AJC. Tannenbaum, who once approached me about being his assistant, gave an account of a recent tour he made of six or seven ghettos across the country. "Didn't you hear?" I turned to the man next to me and said, "Europe is out this year. *The* place to go is the ghettos."

He didn't appreciate my humor.

June 14

At the reception after a bar mitzvah today, I met the grandfather of the bar mitzvah boy. He is in the medicine-cabinet business.

"I've hung in the White House," he told me.

In the evening, I conducted an extraordinary wedding, a marriage by catering hall. It took place in a marriage palace called Cordon Bleu, which is overdecorated in early Miami Jewish. Four other weddings were scheduled simultaneously on the premises, and when I arrived, the doorman asked me, "Which affair, sir?"

I told him.

"Third door on the right," he said.

We went through the preliminary rehearsal and in walked a little man, five feet tall, wearing a *yarmulke*. "I'm Reverend so-and-so," he said. "I come with the catering hall." He warned me that the place was strictly, strictly kosher and that I would have to meet certain requirements, like wearing a *yarmulke*, which I rarely do. I put one on; I figured it couldn't hurt me, and I preferred a skull cap to an argument.

A few minutes later, Reverend so-and-so appeared fully robed, started his ceremonial singing, paused to let me read the ceremony, then sang a few more songs and ended the service. He then took care of the license and proceeded to the next wedding, presumably the fourth room on the right.

June 17

Judith's parents went home to South Carolina today, and before they left they told me they were confident Judith would be back to normal in no time. Her condition is very much improved, and she is now, at a much more relaxed pace, tending to all her household functions. I have been helping her out wherever I can, mostly by spending a lot of time with Sally.

Two ladies who work for Al Lowenstein (one is his executive secretary and the other is a woman with whom he went to law school) came to my house this afternoon. I have been very critical of Al in numerous private conversations in the past few months, and I'm certain he dispatched the women to calm me down.

My primary gripe with Lowenstein is that he has spread himself too thin and those to whom his real commitment is—his constituents—are suffering as a result. But because I am something of a conglomerate of commitments myself, I can understand that what got him into this situation is not a lack of sincerity, but simply an inability to assign priorities.

The ladies were very tactful. They said they had heard that the rabbi was not happy with the Congressman.

"I hope you understand that it's not his political position that I am at odds with," I said. "It's his style."

I told them that every time I had the occasion to seek his help, he never did anything. They insisted, however, that Al was more concerned with the community than I realized. Perhaps they are right. Their very presence, even though politically inspired, is testimony that Lowenstein is trying to make the move back to reality.

"One wonders," I told the ladies, "if Al's constant running around isn't an attempt to avoid a certain degree of self-analysis."

They accused me of talking like Al's rabbi.

As soon as the ladies left, Judith came rushing into my study to tell me that there had been an urgent call from some rabbi, and he had asked that I call him back immediately. I did, and he identified himself as the Far Rockaway chairman of the

Jewish Defense League, which is, in my mind, a lunatic organization formed at the time of the teachers' strike to be a militant counter-group to the fantasy of black anti-Semitism. (I call them the Jewish Weathermen.) He said he had to see me right away.

He arrived shortly afterward, a man in his mid-thirties, wearing a *yarmulke.* (Later, he told me that he had been an Orthodox rabbi at one time, but now sold insurance in ghetto areas.) He said he had received information that a "Get the Jews Day" was planned for today at Lawrence High School. He assumed, he said, that the blacks were arranging it. He said his sources told him there would be violence, rioting, and maybe even bloodshed. As he spoke, I could see him almost mystically conjuring up a lovely pogrom.

In his presence, I made a few calls, the first to the Hot Line, a rumor clinic which had been set up by the Five Towns Coalition. They hadn't heard anything. Next I called the school principal. He said no such thing had occurred or was about to occur.

By the time the insurance-agent-rabbi left my home, school had let out, and the black students had not brought off "Get the Jews Day." My visitor looked disappointed.

June 18

Judith and I went into the city tonight to see the Broadway show, *Plaza Suite.* As we were driving home, she turned to me and said, "Martin, I want you to know I feel so much better. So relieved."

With summer, the pace of my activities will be slacking off, and I'll be able to spend more time with her. She is improving, but not yet well. I'm afraid that it would not take much to trigger a relapse.

June 20

The worship season at Temple Sinai begins in the autumn with the High Holy Days and ends with the start of summer. Because tonight was the next-to-last evening service of this season, I used it as the occasion for my annual "summing up" sermon.

I prefaced what I had to say by reiterating my view that the synagogue is becoming an anachronistic institution, that the style of the Jewish community is changing and that, therefore, it eventually will require a new kind of institution to serve it. The best we can do is die gracefully, not fighting, but yielding to, even encouraging, the coming of the new forms around which the new institution will develop. In this context, in coming to Temple Sinai two years ago, I was determined not to work for the preservation of the synagogue—that would only be a futile exercise—but to help it in the last days move toward relevance so that those who will be shaping the new institution will have at least something of a foundation on which to build. If I could help transform the synagogue into even a transitory vehicle of experimentation, then the new form will be encouraged to consider those elements of the past, those elements of tradition, which represent the wisdom of the human experience, while rejecting those that seemingly survived only for the sake of survival.

Specifically, my goals at Temple Sinai have been to bring adult education to a lèvel of new importance, to revamp the approach to child education and make Judaism relevant to the kids, to move the synagogue into the area of social action, and to create a forum for meaningful, not automatic, worship.

There has been some progress, certainly more than in the average synagogue. Adult-education programs have been expanded, and more members are attending. The religious school has been updated. But we have yet to move significantly in social-action programs, and the mode of worship, the style of prayer, remains wedded to old forms.

The summation was a very personal experience for me, because I am now seriously considering leaving Temple Sinai and perhaps the rabbinate altogether. The lonely travail of Judith's illness has given me a very bitter assessment of my own impact. What is religion if it is not community? What are religious people if they are not people who take a genuine interest in one another, people who can feel and show they feel, people who can care and show they care?

I can recall an experience in Wheeling when Judith burned her arm while baking some rolls. The following morning, a very wealthy eighty-year-old woman, the matriarch of the congregation, arrived at our home in her chauffeured car, woke us up and announced: "I've come to make you breakfast." This could never happen here. Wheeling is a community. The Five Towns is a place where people live.

Here I am with a congregation of three hundred families—all supposedly friendly, kind, intelligent, and devoted to the ideals of Judaism. I have a problem. The Rabbi has a problem. His wife needs friendship; she needs to see that people are really concerned for her. But not a single person—not one—has yet visited us, has yet offered to help us, has yet even called us. Who are these people? What kind of life do they live? What are they doing coming to a synagogue at all? What could it possibly mean to them?

Slowly, I am beginning to recognize my position. I am only their public property. They pay me to be instantly available;

they pay me to lead them in acting out their abstract sense of religion; they pay me to bar mitzvah their sons, marry their children and conduct their funerals. I'm not a human being. I'm an institution. A symbol. A walking, talking, superhuman neo-divine reality.

I am also a janitor. Tonight when I arrived at the Masonic Temple, where we are still holding our services, I was thinking deeply about the sermon, the congregation, and Judith. I guess I was a few minutes late and an officer of the temple came rushing over to me.

"Rabbi, why the hell aren't the chairs set up yet?" he shouted.

June 21

Some of my neighbors staged a block party this afternoon. Each family contributed $10, a rock band was hired, the street was closed off, and colored lights were draped from the telephone poles. There were games for the children and games for the adults, and we all hauled our charcoal grills out to the sidewalk, where together we grilled and traded hamburgers.

I talked to a lot of faces I had seen on the street the past few years, and, in a sense, I guess we all got to know one another

But for what? Next year's block party?

June 22

I conducted two unveiling ceremonies at two different cemeteries today, and I had to operate on a split-second schedule to get to both on time.

The first unveiling was for the mother of the gentleman who had interviewed me to determine whether I had the appropriate social conscience to conduct the ceremony. I met the family and talked with them and found them to be very charming and alert people. I'll probably never see them again, however, because that's the way it is with rabbis: No deposit, no return. Use and dispose.

The second unveiling was a very unpleasant experience. The mother of a young man who had died accused me of not putting her son's name on the memorial plaque at the temple.

"We don't usually do that unless we are asked to," I said. I didn't mention that there's a charge of $100.

"You are not taking proper care of my son's memory, Rabbi," she said.

June 23

To my utter surprise, Judith and I were invited at the last minute to dinner tonight at the home of a member of my congregation. Judith was thrilled. We had a pleasant time, and I think the evening is going to help quicken her recovery.

June 24

Several months ago, I talked to a couple who were feuding over whether to have a $15,000 bar mitzvah for their son. The father said he couldn't afford it and didn't want it. The mother said she wanted it whether the father could afford it or not. I urged her to have a small modest affair.

"That will take courage, Rabbi," she said, "but I'll try."

She called me today to tell me that she had decided on a gala $15,000 spectacular.

"You'll drive your husband to bankruptcy," I said.

"But at least we'll be able to face our neighbors," she replied.

The library in the community has been running a film called *The Answer,* which is about a riddle and one man's attempt to solve it. The riddle embodies all the problems of mankind and its solution, we find out in the end, is no less than the Ten Commandments.

Tonight I was invited to speak after the film. I told the group that I didn't believe in abstract universals like the Ten Commandments.

The librarian was very upset.

June 25

A student who attended our Five Towns Coalition meeting tonight said to me afterward, "Why do you deal with organizations? Why don't you deal with people?"

It was a good question, because I think it pinpoints the difficulty we're having in getting any of our projects moving. We are a super-organization made up of representatives of other organizations such as the American Jewish Congress, the League of Women Voters and the National Council of Jewish Women. Each of these member organizations has its own vested interests, and the coalition, while it should be acting as a vehicle through which they combine their efforts, has instead become a battleground where they fight to carve out their own absolute jurisdictions.

An organization is an abstraction, a façade around which human reality is expressed. Therefore, the coalition, which is an organization of organizations, is an *abstract* organization with utterly no reality except its own abstraction.

It's funny that I should be its president—now that I think of it—because in my other life, as a rabbi, I am an abstraction myself. No matter how much I seek out personal relationships, people only view me as an object. I am supposed to sit above it all, on a celestial pedestal, contemplating large things, while all the worldly people below come to me, drop coins in the slot and have their Jewishness serviced.

I am not considered a *Jew,* but *Judaism* itself. I am not expected to be a human being. I am not allowed to be a human being.

And who most of all does not allow me to be a human being? Me. I don't allow it. I am a rabbi, and I must live with the reality that unless people have confidence in me on the pulpit I cannot be effective. Therefore, in everything I want to do, I must first assess whether in doing it I will be destroying the confidence my congregation has in me.

The other day I wanted to buy a pair of bell-bottom trousers. I didn't. Why? Because a congregation does not *expect* its rabbi to wear bell-bottom trousers. I think at heart I'm a swinger, but I will never let myself swing. I can count many occasions when I've wanted to cry, or laugh, or be sarcastic, or be affectionate, or be silly, but I couldn't. It wasn't *expected* of me. So I just repressed what might have been natural and instead did whatever was appropriate.

So all of the insulation and all of the isolation from which I now suffer is as much my doing as anybody else's. Long ago I should have made my stand: *I will be myself. I will not live up to your role expectations. I, like you, am human. Take me for what I am or don't take me at all.*

I'm thinking of taking my stand now—on the contract. Whether or not it's proper, I want more money. A lot more money. They have plenty of money to build their supersanctuary, and yet I've been getting paid less than I should. Everybody is out for himself in this community, and since that's the case, I'm going to start looking out for myself, too. I want more money. If they won't give it to me, I'll leave.

June 27

Tonight was our last Friday evening service of the worship season and three students from Cornell who are members of the congregation came to discuss the racial situation on campus. There was such a good and hearty exchange between the students and the congregation that I postponed the coffee-and-cake gathering which is usually held immediately after the service. This affronted one of the congregants.

"The bar mitzvah family paid for their coffee and cake, and they are entitled to serve it," she said to me afterward.

"I'm sorry," I said, "but I won't be held captive to fifteen dollars worth of coffee and cake."

June 28

I have received a number of phone calls from people who are not members of my congregation who would like me to perform weddings. But I have decided, in light of Judith's illness, that to involve myself in these things would not be a valid expenditure of my time. I turned them all down. I have also hired an answering service for my telephone to relieve Judith of another burden. She continues to be fragile, and I am determined to do everything I can to keep her life at a manageable pace.

When I first moved to Woodmere, the mother of a boy who was having serious psychiatric problems came to see me. Her son, because of his condition, was unable to attend religious school, but he had told her that he would like to have a bar mitzvah like everyone else.

I had been warned about this woman. She had enrolled two other sons in the religious school, then withdrew them the day after their bar mitzvahs, which around here is considered a confession of pure exploitation, and it affronted some of the old-liners in the congregation. Most boys who are bar mitzvah at least finish out the year in religious school and many continue for another year. I had been advised by certain members that if this woman approaches me, I should simply cite the rule that nobody can have a bar mitzvah unless he attends religious school.

But when I talked to the woman I found her warm, friendly and sincere. I thought her situation was credible, so I told her that we would bend the rules for her son.

This morning the young man had his bar mitzvah, and he did a marvelous job. Having proved to himself that he can do as well and better than other boys his age, he has found a self-assurance he never before had. He told me before the service that next year he wanted to go to religious school to learn more about Judaism.

For the first time since I've been in the Five Towns, a Christian delegation visited our services today. They were a group of Lutherans visiting New York from throughout the country who had expressed an interest in attending a Jewish service.

In Wheeling, where Jews are very sensitive about their position with Gentiles, visits like this were a regular occurrence.

They had reason to be sensitive. One time I remember a visiting young Christian asking, "Rabbi, where is the place you sacrifice the animals?"

June 30

A few years ago, when I was living in Wheeling, I remember seeing a pamphlet distributed by the Anti-Defamation League. It was one of a series called *Your Neighbor Celebrates,* and the purpose was to show Christians that their Jewish neighbors were no different from them. The pamphlet went on to explain that, except for a few dissimilar beliefs, the Jewish religion was like any Christian religion. I remember reading something to the effect that "You Christians go to church; we go to the synagogue. You hold up the crucifix; we hold up the Torah."

Shortly after I saw this pamphlet, the Six-Day War took place in the Middle East, and the ADL propaganda fell from the sky as quickly as Egyptian MIGs. Christians began asking themselves: *Why should my Jewish neighbors, who are the same as I am except that they worship a little differently, care so much about this little country thousands of miles away?*

Those events prompted me to set up a summer institute where Christians could learn about Jews and where the emphasis would be on teaching Judaism, not apologizing for it. Jews *are* different, despite the ADL's efforts to excuse us for it, and Jewishness is more than a religion. I realized that if there were ever going to be any genuine interreligious communication, somebody had to start telling Christians the truth about Judaism, whether it was what they wanted to hear or not.

The first institute took place at Wheeling College in 1967. It was such a success that it was held again last summer. This year its format has been copied by a number of other interested groups, and there will be a total of eight such institutes going on across the country. For all but one, I will serve as general chairman.

That one exception is an institute to be held at Seton Hall University. It's financed and sponsored by the ADL. The person in charge of the program contacted me earlier this year and said, "We ask you not to attend."

"I won't," I said. "But I'm sorry you feel so threatened."

This summer I'll actually attend two of the institutes, one in August at Grailville in Ohio, the other at Marymount College in Tarrytown, New York, which will begin officially tomorrow.

I arrived in Tarrytown today. Most of the people attending this particular institute are nuns from the New York Archdiocese. They have been anticipating the program enthusiastically and today told me that they would like to hold it next year in the form of a trip to Israel. They said they had heard that the Seton Hall institute was planning its own trip to Israel next summer, and they asked me to call and see if we could make arrangements for a joint pilgrimage.

I called the head of the Seton Hall program today and made the proposal.

"Absolutely not," she said.

July 1

Since Tarrytown is only an hour's ride from my home, I came back last night so Judith would not have to be alone. This morning, as I was driving back to Marymount, I ran a stoplight. A policeman saw me, and signaled me to the side of the road.

"You stupid son of a bitch," he said. "Do you know what you just did?"

His inflection didn't really invite an answer. He asked for my license. When I gave it to him, his face fell.

"Oh, Rabbi," he said, "you must forgive me. I didn't know you were a rabbi. You must have been thinking great thoughts."

He was serious. He let me go without a ticket.

July 2

I am devoting my lectures at this Marymount seminar, and the seminar later this summer at Grailville, to a discussion of the possibility that we are now entering a Jewish Century, a time when the spirit of community, the nonideological blend of the emotional and the rational, and the resistance to categories and forms, will all emerge through the forces of antinationalism to provide us with a new kind of society. I call the process the Judaization of Christianity, because Christianity will be the vehicle through which the society becomes Jewish.

The process has already begun. There has been a rekindling of interest, mostly among the young, in the nonrational, nontheological mystique of the Eastern religions. At the same time, the Western state is under attack, as evidenced here in America, where legions of the young are refusing to acknowledge its ultimate authority in manipulating their lives.

In the midst of all these changes, Judaism, a synthesis of Eastern tradition which never paid much attention to nationalism in the first place, will find itself in the unique position of providing the religious form for the direction in which the world is shifting. For this reason, I feel that in the years to come Judaism will no longer necessarily have its home in the Jewish people, but in all people who seek a religious response to their existence.

Today's youth—as adults—will be the people who shape the Jewish Century because, unlike their parents, they are a generation free of ideology. At present they only frighten the older generation who, like Nixon for example, feel control is very important, and that life should be lived in a highly logical, systematic and programmed manner, based on the logic, systems and programs of their own invention. They see the kids as a threat to their value system. At a time like this, Nixon is probably President, among other reasons, because his daughter, Tricia, can stand up in the White House and be a youthful voice reassuring America that "God is good and God is great," which is the typical middle-class Protestant ethic. Tricia, of course, is not typical; she is a remnant of a passing age, and so is her father. They represent those people who are frightened and who are holding on in growing desperation to a way of life which is disappearing. They are not Christians. They are Gentiles. Their God is the state.

Nixon's America is just another place the Jews have lived. Among the oldest of civilizations, the Jews were in Babylonia, in Egypt, in Rome and in Greece. In each instance, these early cultures were capsulated and modified in Judaism—not always perfectly, because the Jews themselves were at best imperfect vehicles. Yet, at least since the fourth century B.C. and probably before that, the Jews have been a world people. Today our modern concept of utopia is an international *community,* which the Jews have already had amorphously for 1,600 years.

Civilization has often lagged a few paces behind the nationless Jews. When slavery was widely practiced in Biblical times, for instance, the Jews enforced only a moderate, humane form of it. The Jews in the Bible called for each man to give up his worldly possessions and start over every fifty years, and for all debts to be canceled every seven years. Sick funds and welfare funds have existed among Jews for centuries. Jewish prophets have always taught that God was involved with ethics, not politics, and that nationhood was not to be glorified into a divine state.

Now, after centuries of trailing the Jews, civilization is catching up. The Jews have realized the opportunity to join, and are joining, the Establishment. Many Jews have so Westernized themselves that they have created an unfortunate new breed of Jewish Gentiles. This leads me to believe that the true Christians will probably become the new Jews.

How?

In their efforts to assimilate, the Jews have undergone two major processes. The first was religious adaptation, reforming Judaism so that it would relate to the life-style of the nation in which any particular community of Jews lived. Thus, we have English Jews, Italian Jews and American Jews, meaning that the Jews accept nationalistic expression, which is the dominant theme of modern society.

Then came the statehood of Israel, the ultimate nationalistic expression of the Jews. Where religious adaptation essentially failed as a method of assimilation, because it was only a meager concession to a world which operated on nationalistic principles, Israel really moved the Jews into modern society. It is now the God of many Jews, just as America is the God of Nixon and the Gentiles. The Jewish community outside Israel, as years pass, is not likely to survive in its present form, because it is basically vestigial. The modern reality of Judaism for most Jews is in the nationalism of the state of Israel.

Simultaneous to these developments, Christianity has come to find itself a victim of the modern concept of the state. From medieval times up until a few centuries ago, nations themselves were Christian, dominated by a Christian morality and operating on a structure based upon God's will. The state was able to enforce God's morality, a morality it designed to suit its own needs. Wars were holy, laws were sacred, virtually everything was crried out in the name of God. The Christian hierarchy was an integral part of the political leadership.

But then the world began to change its complexion, and the power of Christianity diminished. America was founded in a framework in which church and state were separate. In communist nations, a new power took over the position once occupied by the church. In Western Europe, where Christianity was once universal, people began to view their Christian identity much less seriously.

What does all this mean? It means that Christianity has become again what it once was within Judaism—a minority. It is no longer capable of forming the world to its will. More powerful forces prevail and control the society. It means that the Christian, if the Jewish experience is any guide, can expect to be persecuted if he acts on the basis of his beliefs, since what he believes is often likely to be regarded as a threat to the underpinnings of the national society.

The nature of the persecution varies with the state. In the Soviet Union, at one extreme, the Christian is persecuted outright, simply for his existence. The communist goal is the annihilation of the church. In America, the situation is more complex. From the moment the nation was founded, God was divorced from nationhood. The church never held power in America, it never had official influence and it was never used as an instrument to enforce the national morality.

Therefore, from the start, America developed into a homogenized secular-religious society, with the Christian church part of the establishment, but never a direct instrument of power. The society was never officially motivated by Christian attitudes;

it merely retained certain pietisms, such as benedictions, invoca tions, prayers in Congress, the chaplaincy in the military, and the entire self-image of a churchgoing people.

But in lieu of God, the will of the people became the instrument to enforce the Christian morality. America, therefore, became its own religion, and the American religion swallowed up Christianity. Christianity was used by the general society for whatever needs it might have: *Praise the Lord, pass the ammunition.* Wars and laws, although not Christian, were in themselves holy to the American religion.

This is where the Gentiles and the Christians separate. The Gentile worships the American religion, his country right or wrong. He is in the majority. He has joined the nation, not the religious community, and prefers to worship the state while calling himself a Christian. His values have no religious dimension; they are formed by the secular society to suit its own needs. The Gentile subscribes to a particular set of values whose purpose is simply the preservation of the state.

The Christian, on the other hand, may often find himself differing from that which the nation requires, and, as such, he is in the minority. As long as his conscience leads him to differ with the state—which it must at times, because the Christian teachings really do not glorify nationalism—he will be unable to accept the state's sacred secular ideology. Therefore, the Christian is the object of persecution, interestingly enough not only from the state, but from the official church itself which, as part of the establishment, is in the position of having to support the state.

How is he persecuted? For one thing, the Christian (unlike the Gentile), in rejecting nationalism as an ultimate value, is likely to oppose the war in Vietnam. Since his opposition is on Christian terms, he is persecuted, sometimes tormented, and sometimes even jailed. The *official* ideology sympathizes only with conscientious objectors from religions which *officially* reject war. If an individual Christian refuses to serve in the Army, he has to prove to his draft board that he is doing so for more than the fact that he's a Christian. The conscience of a Christian in America is not in itself a valid license to oppose the social doctrine.

Christians who have opposed the military draft are in jail or in exile. Christians were persecuted in Chicago in 1968. Christians are persecuted today on campuses and in the streets and in the courts.

The Gentiles have taken over. Any man who opposes the various acts of oppression carried out in the name of the American religion is persecuted.

Enter the Jews. They have been through it all before. For many thousands of years, Judaism has been the religious response of the minority. Wherever Jews lived, they could assume that the society would be at its worst flagrantly antagonistic and at its best indifferent toward them. They had to assume that their style of life, the teachings and customs of their religion, their values and their ideals, would, at a minimum, receive no support from the society. Furthermore, the Jews had to face the reality (until Israel was made a Jewish state) that there was no place in the world where they could feel at home. Now, as Christianity becomes a minority belief among Gentiles, Christians, in order to survive, will have to start operating like Jews. They will have to develop a life-style which has been until now associated with the world's most experienced persecuted minority, the Jews.

Through its minority experience, one of the things which has kept Judaism alive has been its commitment to prophecy. Because prophecy assures ultimate authenticity to an individual no matter what, it is the ultimate response of any persecuted religious minority. Furthermore, an entire people can think of themselves in terms of a prophetic role, through which they confirm their own separateness by invoking the authority of prophecy. A prophet says: "I have experienced God and that experience tells me that I am not wrong. Who cares who disagrees with me? I have it on the highest authority, which is available only to me, that I am right. I am a minority of one. I am my own authenticity."

When it first began as a minority, Christianity was very much involved with prophecy, but when its prophetic visions threatened the existence of the state in which the Christian hierarchy by that time was participating, prophecy was branded un-Christian. In the Jewish Christianity of the next century, however, Christians will be coming back to prophecy to support their own authenticity in the face of an unfriendly nationalistic society.

A minority can survive outside the structure of the state only if it maintains its own sense of community. Without community, there would be no Judaism, a fact easily evidenced today because as the Jewish community is finally disintegrating, so is modern Judaism. A minority must survive as an internal community, no matter how amorphous it is. The reality of Judaism has never been in a formal state or governmental structure but in the Jews themselves, dispersed around the world, yet caring for one another in community.

Just as early, minority Christianity was prophetic, it was also community-centered. But then with the conversion of the Emperor Constantine, Christianity became a part of the government and its internal community no longer had reason to exist. Now the Gentiles are the majority and their religion is the state religion, and for the Christians to survive, they must again become a community, like the Jews.

Because the Jewish community, a dispersed minority, never had a formal structure in which to operate, its legal traditions were virtually unenforceable from high above. Therefore, the Jews had to make allowances for diversity within unity. This was provided by the local community. All laws were subject ultimately to individual local interpretation, and what became authentically legal was not the letter of the law, but the way it was interpreted locally. The interpretation took on all the authority and authenticity of the original law. The law became both adjustable and authoritative, divine and contemporary. It was this crucial adjustment which provided the heart of the Jewish experience in its minority situation.

Judaism learned early that only in allowing diversity would intramural squabbles which undermine unity be avoided. The *Talmud,* which is the authoritative compilation of post-Biblical Jewish traditions, is made up of the *Mishna* and the *Gamora.* The *Mishna* is essentially the earliest post-Biblical traditions and the *Gamora* the varied interpretations of them. The *Gamora* reads as if it were a group interview, like shorthand notes of conversation. Everybody has his own interpretation and each, so to speak, is the law, although in some instances one interpretation is the accepted version.

Christianity, and especially Catholicism, has traditionally attempted to enforce worldwide the letter of its religious law. Only recently has a slight decentralizing process begun through which at least some allowance is made for individual interpretation. Much of the ferment within the Christian sects today is a result of those who believe that the church can still teach and enforce universally acceptable values, and those who realize that now, as a minority, it cannot. Obviously only a truly universal church can make its view of truth binding. A non-universal church can only speak for itself, and its members for themselves, if it is to survive as a religious institution at all.

This means that in America, for instance, only Gentiles have the mechanisms to enforce the American religion. Christianity, on the other hand, no longer has the political means of backing up its own authority against the competing ideology of the Gentiles. Therefore, the Christian minority, like the Jewish minority before it, will have to establish a legal tradition to allow for its own dissent and diversity.

Another major change in Christianity as it responds to its minority situation will be in the nature of its institution. The church will become more like a synagogue in concept, an expression of the community and not of the institutional hierarchy. Similarly, the ideology will become more diverse, tolerating differences of opinion which do not undermine, but promote the unity.

The process when completed will be the Judaization of Christianity. It will be a new religious form which is neither Judaism nor Christianity. A community of people experiencing one another will be at its base. They will be neither Christian Gentiles who worship the state nor Jewish Gentiles who worship Israel; they will be the *real* Christians and the *real* Jews who have come together.

The theologies and beliefs which now separate Christians from Jews will be irrelevant. Each man may have his own mind. The reality will be in communication. The reality will be in understanding that religion is man's interest in things not of the moment, his concern with that which has been and that which will be and that which is in the depths of existing things. Religion, as it will be understood, will be only the dimension through which man can see longer, deeper and wider.

Whether this new religious form of Judaized Christianity becomes the dominant force in the society depends on what happens to the concept of the national state. If the Gentiles are eventually outnumbered, nationhood will lose its force, and a world community could emerge with Judaized Christianity as its appropriate religious expression: a unification of all diversity without uniformity.

And if we can't achieve a world community?

Then I don't imagine we'll be a world much longer.

July 3

Everybody has been discussing my theory on the Judaization of Christianity. The comments have been favorable, and nobody has challenged me. Since the theory represents years of thinking, and since I hope it will be the subject of a future book, I'm obviously very happy.

July 4

I followed Allard Lowenstein as a speaker at an Independence Day peace rally in Cedarhurst this afternoon. I was determined not to utter the usual Fourth of July pomposities. Instead, I spoke to a feeling that meant something to me, and I really didn't care what people thought.

"The Fourth of July is a holiday to celebrate America," I said, "but I wonder: who owns America? Does it belong to those people who build great armies with which they fight useless wars and through which they pervert democracy? Does it belong to those American Legionnaires who parade down the streets of the nation this afternoon after they struggled all morning to get into uniforms which no longer fit?

"These are not the people who really own America," I said. "Today is not their holiday. It is a holiday for those of us who are seeking to make America what it is supposed to be, for those of us who oppose this war and those of us who fight the military. We *are* America. We stand for its true ideal."

Afterward, a Cornell student who wore beads and peace

buttons asked me if I thought *we* could really trust America, if there was any hope left for his generation.

I told him what it was like to be in college during the McCarthy era. "America is far from what we would like it to be," I said, "but even today it is far more than it was ten years ago."

July 5

I'm on vacation this month, and today I just loafed, swimming in the pool, resting and reading.

I didn't even go to Saturday-morning services.

July 8

At 8:30 this evening, the phone rang. Bob Mandel was calling. "Where are you, Rabbi?" he asked. "Aren't you coming to the meeting?"

"What meeting?"

"The meeting we called to discuss your contract."

I had forgotten all about it.

I dressed quickly, a little shaken because, despite the importance of this moment, I had not yet worked out my strategy.

When I arrived, the board of trustees told me that my future had been discussed by the executive committee and it was "generally agreed" that they wanted me to continue as rabbi. Mandel said, however, that there had been some criticisms of me, and that he felt he had to inform me of them before we discussed the details of the contract.

"The main criticism we have of you," he said, "is that you don't seem to care about the details of people's lives. To be quite blunt, Rabbi, you don't pay enough attention to people."

I erupted inside.

"Well, that's probably true," I said. "I'm not a good pastor and I have never billed myself as one. When I don't know somebody, I can't get very concerned if he has a hernia."

There are people in this congregation I never see, but when they get sick, they like to be visited. I suppose I should visit them; in fact, I know I should, I feel I should. But I can't be a phony. I can't be a stiff, professional friend who goes out and makes a house call because somebody in the congregation is sick and feels he is entitled to a visit by the rabbi. I would do anything in the world for the people I know and care for. But for the others whom I don't know, I can't. I realize it's part of my job, and that I should do it, but I detest doing it so much, I usually put it off until it's too late.

"But as long as you brought up the subject," I said, "maybe I should tell all of you something. I've had a problem in my family with Judith for two and a half months, and not a single person has made even the slightest gesture to help. Even though there's been a constant tension operating in my household, nobody in this vast congregation has shown the least bit of concern. I don't see why I should be a friend to people who don't give a damn about me."

I sat down, and for a few moments, the room was silent.

"To tell the truth, Rabbi," somebody finally spoke up in a very decent tone of voice, "I didn't know. I honestly didn't know that Judith was ill."

A few others said the same thing.

"That could be my fault," Mandel said. "I did know about it, and I didn't tell anybody. I didn't feel it was a proper thing to talk about."

I was still steaming. "I'm like a service-station attendant," I said. "If you need my services, I'm available. This is what you pay me for—to conduct your bar mitzvahs, your weddings, and your funerals. This is my job, and to most of you it's my entire job. Truthfully, I can't see any point in entering the personal fabric of your lives if you don't care to have me there, or if you don't care to make any effort to enter the personal fabric of my life. You know, there's not a single individual in this congregation I could call a friend."

"We never made any effort to be friendly with you," one man said, "because we figured you didn't want to talk about the temple all the time, and when we get together, the temple seems to be all we talk about."

Since I had not spoken to hear apologies, I didn't dwell any further on the subject.

I nodded at the man and continued. "Now about the contract," I said. "When I came here, I felt, as I still do, that the synagogue as an institution was in great trouble. My hope was that I could renovate Temple Sinai, that I could modernize it. There have been many, many frustrations, but I do feel—or at least I would like to feel—that some progress has been made."

I knew what I was about to say, and yet I hadn't even decided to say it. It was an odd feeling. Had I been playing games with myself all these months? Had I ever intended to leave? "And I guess," I heard myself saying, "that this progress, however minimal, warrants my continuing on the job." I paused. "That is, if you find my conditions acceptable."

"Well, what are your conditions?" Bob Mandel asked.

"For one thing, more money," I said. "My main concern now is that I am not living off my salary. I have other investments and a teaching job at Woodmere Academy, without either of which I would not be able to survive. I want to make enough money to live off my salary alone. The amount you now pay me is unrealistic."

"How much money are we talking about?" Mandel asked.

"This year my basic salary is $17,000. I want an immediate raise to $20,000, and then yearly increments of $1,000 each up to $25,000 on a five-year contract."

Mandel immediately opposed a five-year contract. The standard term of contract in the congregation has been three years. He told me that, because the economy was so unpredictable, a long-term contract would be a gamble not only for them, but for me. Somebody suggested as a compromise a five-year contract with renegotiation after three years. I said I'd probably agree to something like that.

"I also want one specific provision written into the contract," I said. "If the membership of the congregation exceeds a certain level, I want to be allowed to resign."

"What do you mean?" Mandel said. "What we're trying to do right now is increase the membership to help pay for the building."

"I'm well aware of that," I said, "but it's bad enough to be an attendant in a service station. I have no intention of becoming a foreman in a factory. I believe the heart of Judaism is in personal relationships—even though I have so few of them. If the membership gets beyond a certain point, the need for my services at weddings, bar mitzvahs, and funerals will grow so great that I won't have any time left to get involved with people. Nor will I have the freedom to do the other things I want to do. I have no desire to be a rabbi under those circumstances."

Mandel said the executive committee would examine my request for this "unusual" provision in the contract, and would make a spot check on rabbis' salaries in comparably-sized congregations in the area. He said they would have a reaction to my terms at a later meeting.

In all, it was a gentlemanly, honest, open—if indeterminate—session. I guess the reason I decided to offer to renew my contract is something that has been operating in the back of my mind all this time: I have nothing better to do which will pay me $20,000 a year.

I got home quite late and Judith was up waiting for me. She was very excited. She wanted to know what had happened. I didn't tell her what I had said about her illness. If people do begin to show some concern for her, I don't want her to be suspicious.

July 9

Judith and I drove into the city and saw a matinee performance of *1776*, the Broadway musical. The show was enjoyable—and an emotional release for both of us. When we drove home, we felt closer than we'd felt in a long time.

July 10

A member of my congregation, Al Vorspan, has written a book called *My Rabbi Doesn't Make House Calls,* which will soon be published by Doubleday. Al, who is the director of social action for the Union of American Hebrew Congregations, is a dynamic leader of Reform Judaism. Despite the fact that I am his rabbi, the book has nothing to do with me. It is an anecdotal account of professional Jewish organizations, such as the UAHC, a collection of vignettes, some of them tongue-in-cheek, from his life as a professional Jew. Today he called me to find out if I had any objection to the title.

"We just want to be sure," he said, "because the publishers are concerned that since you *are* my rabbi, there may be some confusion."

"I don't think there's any problem, Al," I said, "but you'll have to come over here to discuss it. I don't make house calls."

July 12

I attended services this morning and found them peaceful, meaningful and relaxing—when I'm not conducting them.

July 13

I received a letter six months ago inviting me to participate in something called the Institute of Man and Science at Rensselaer, New York. Until the moment I stepped off the plane in Albany this afternoon, where representatives from the institute met me, I didn't have the slightest idea what the institute was or what was expected of me. All I knew was that I was to be paid $50 a day.

After nearly an hour's drive from Albany, we reached the country estate where the Institute is being held. I was greeted as "a member of the faculty," with a dozen or so "nice to have you's." I sat down to dinner in a lavish dining room, and my tablemates included an abstract sociologist, a rabbi who kept talking about psycho-religious drama, a lawyer, and a few business executives. I found out that the theme of the institute would be "Family and Kind."

We moved from the dining room to a conference room, and the show was on. A peculiar combination of people attended, mostly retirees and high-school students, hardly anyone over twenty and under sixty.

One of the "faculty members" spoke about race relations, another about a settlement house in Philadelphia and the psycho-religious rabbi gave his views on nudity in the theater. I stuck to the theme and spoke for a few minutes on the social structure and how it was causing changes in the nature of the family.

After a short question-and-answer period, I went to my assigned room, called Judith, and fell asleep.

July 14

The second day of the institute opened with one faculty member discussing "Puerto Rican and Negro Life-Styles," which turned out to be mostly a detailed description of how he had to hitchhike to the conference because his car broke down. The man who spoke about race relations last night spoke about race relations again, and the rabbi had more to say on nudity in the theater. To be different, I spoke on the future of the family.

Afterward, a seventy-year-old woman whose grandson had married a Jew came up to inform me that I was brilliant, unusual, interesting, and charming. Then she shadowed me for the rest of the day. Toward evening, she suggested, "Why don't we go to Israel together? I'll pay." I guess she thought that's the way to pick up a rabbi.

In the evening, the other rabbi finally staged his psycho-religious drama. Most of the drama was when would he stop talking. His main point was that we have to be honest and open in interpersonal relationships and that nudity helps us to achieve this. He employed his audience as actors. He was show business all the way. His whole spectacle was rather sad and pitiful and a distortion of what human relationship is all about. Besides, nobody was nude.

July 15

The psycho-religio rabbi asked if he could take a few minutes this morning to probe our reactions to his non-nude nudity drama. He probed for two hours. He was followed by a woman from UNICEF who managed to cover thirty to forty topics in as many minutes, none of which, of course, related to anything. Then I was asked to say a "few words" on the Jewish family style. I said, "The Jewish family is child-centered and material-centered," and left it at that.

In the evening, a well-known sex expert arrived in a Rolls Royce with her husband, who was obviously the junior partner in the relationship. She gave the keynote address in which she told us, profoundly and expensively, that sex is more than fornication.

If it weren't for the $50 a day, I'd go home tonight.

July 16

The topic of the family could be a very interesting one, but nobody at this conference wants to discuss it. Today, instead, we discussed male homosexuality, lesbianism, and other aberrations, and everybody announced that he preferred the normal husband-wife-child thing.

I couldn't care less what these people prefer.

July 17

The conference broke up this morning, not a minute too soon, and I hurried home to Woodmere, took a swim and went to bed, $200 richer.

There must be better ways to make a living.

July 18

I got a letter today from my second alma mater, Hebrew Union College. When I was a student there, even if you finished the full five-year graduate course, you didn't receive a master's degree—unless you took a special exam. I didn't take the exam. I didn't get the degree.

But the letter today offered me the master's degree simply for signing a form and returning it "along with $25." The school had belatedly determined that every graduate was entitled to the degree, whether he'd taken the exam or not.

I'm not going to send them $25. Why should I?

I conferred the degree on myself a long time ago.

July 20

At the second of two weddings I conducted today, I had to delay the ceremony because someone had persuaded the bride and groom to take their vows at precisely the moment the astronauts' LEM touched down on the moon.

As a relative with a transistor radio whispered, "Five, four, three, two, one," I pronounced the couple man and wife.

July 21

I spent the whole day at home with Judith, who is nearly recovered from her breakdown. She is still not as strong as she was, and no matter how much I help her around the house, I sense that Sally still frustrates her. This frightens me, because, at best, Judith's situation is precarious, and I am in a dilemma. If I spend too much time with Sally, Judith may feel I don't think she is capable of handling the child. Yet, if I don't spend enough time with Sally, Judith could have a relapse.

July 23

Judith and I went to see *Hadrian VII* tonight, a play in which a man sees himself as Pope and writes a book about it. Judith said the play helped her to understand some things about me.

July 25

I went to services as a spectator tonight and afterward mingled with the congregants, thinking about what the board members had said a few weeks ago about me not getting involved in the details of people's lives. I asked one woman how her garden was coming along.

"I live in an apartment," she said.

July 26

A few weeks ago, I got a long-distance phone call from a young couple in St. Louis who wanted me to marry them. They had already been married a year ago by a priest. But the wife, a Catholic, said she wanted her husband, a Jew, to realize his religious heritage. When I spoke to the husband, he seemed less than enthusiastic. This made me leery, but they insisted on coming to New York and meeting with me, anyway.

They showed up today.

"Will you marry us?" the wife asked.

"Why?" I said.

"Because I feel my husband, down deep, is a very religious person."

"Wait a minute," he interrupted. "Down deep, I'm not religious. I am doing this only for your sake."

"But you are . . ."

"I am not, and you know it." He turned to me. "Rabbi, I don't care if you marry us or not," he said. "I'm only doing this for her. I was raised as an Orthodox Jew on the Lower East Side, and, believe me, I have no use for Judaism."

"Well," I asked him, "would you at least be willing to learn and study other kinds of Judaism?"

His wife was almost crying.

"Rabbi," he said, "I only began to live when I got away from New York." Apparently, he equated New York and Judaism, and in getting away from New York, he felt he was getting away from his Jewishness. That probably explained the marriage.

I felt bad for her. She wanted him to exhibit a religious quality, but the most he would accept was a Jewish marriage, and he wouldn't even do that gracefully. He was more than indifferent. He was antagonistic. I wish I could have performed the marriage for her sake, but I felt I couldn't allow Judaism to be abused. "It's probably better to perform no wedding at all," I said, finally, "than to perform a meaningless one. And from what you say, this would be meaningless."

At this point, they both got up, said, "Okay, thank you," and left.

And then I realized that I had said exactly what he had brought her to hear.

July 30

I spent a good part of the day studying for my driver's test. I'm still using a West Virginia license after living here for two years, because I have twice taken and twice failed the New York State written test.

Tomorrow I'm going to take the test once again, but this time I'm going to use a new strategy: Talmudic logic.

July 31

I failed again.

So much for Talmudic logic.

August 1

Last night I dreamt I won the National Book Award for this diary.

My vacation ended tonight, and I returned to the reality of conducting services.

August 2

Judith woke up this morning crying hysterically. She couldn't talk. She could only cry.

I've known all along she hadn't fully recovered from the ordeal in May, but I have no idea what set her off again so suddenly.

She was too ill for me to leave her, so I phoned Bob Mandel and told him I wouldn't be able to conduct services this morning. Then I called Judith's psychiatrist and he prescribed some strong tranquilizers. My mother came out from Brooklyn and spent the day taking care of Sally, while I stayed with Judith and tried to soothe her. Eventually she calmed down, but whenever she tried to talk, tears would overcome her.

"Marty," she said over and over again, "I'm so scared. I'm so worried I am going to have a breakdown."

I can hardly believe this is happening again, and yet why shouldn't it be? Have we really done anything to get at the causes? A few months ago, she complained that I was not available, that I was not spending very much time at home with her and Sally. Since then, of course, I've been with her more. But hasn't this just made her more dependent on me, and more aware of how few friends we have, how alone we are together?

A rabbi is an abstraction, and now, more than ever, I am beginning to feel the awful weight of this abstraction. While I have been able to carry it, I can see that Judith has not. She wants to be human, and people will only allow her to be the wife of an abstraction, an extension of my own unreality.

People tend to make me a symbol. They say they know me, but they don't. They know only my *roles.* To some of them, I am a radical. To some of them, I am the signature on the marriage contract. To some of them, I am the man who opposes the indulgences of the psychotic fear of anti-Semitism. People see me only as they care or need to see me.

And poor Judith has to be the wife to all this.

I can't recognize myself in their eyes, so how could she? We both have to live as exhibits in this community. While people are friendly, we have no friends. We have been made into what they want us to be. Everybody seems to care about us, but yet nobody really does.

It seems that I'm endlessly meeting people—strangers—who say, "I've heard about you. You stand for racial harmony." Or: "You stand for progressive religious education." I have become nothing but a public symbol. I am dissected, examined, interpreted and misunderstood. And Judith? She is prisoner to this reflection. She is allowed no self.

I am dynamic. I am aggressive. I am prophetic. I am concerned. I am lonely.

I want to be what I am, not a symbol of what I am.

I don't want Judith to have to be the wife of a symbol. She's worried about having an emotional breakdown, knowing that I am the only one who cares for her. I am her only friend, if I am that.

All day I kept thinking: A simple phone call from somebody, from anybody, inviting us to dinner, to a party, anywhere, even if we couldn't go, would be better than any medicine a psychiatrist could prescribe.

August 3

My mother is still taking care of Sally, and I have been spending nearly every minute with Judith. She is getting worse, crying more frequently, not functioning at all. She is so fearful of having another breakdown that this self-imposed pressure may actually cause her to have it, if she isn't already having it.

A young couple called today and insisted on coming over, claiming they are having some very difficult problems and need my help. They are engaged and living together; the problem is the girl's mother. The mother is a divorcee, who is bitter toward men, and she and the girl are very close. The mother claims that the young man, who is twenty-three, is a homosexual. Naturally, this has upset the girl and her relationship with the boy.

He does seem somewhat effeminate in his manner of speech, but the fact that they are living together and having sexual relations (sometimes as often as two and three times a night, according to the girl), means to me at least that he is capable of functioning as a heterosexual. He may be trying to prove this to himself.

"Well," I said to him. "Have you ever had homosexual relations?"

"No," he said.

We talked for about half an hour and I told them, essentially, to ignore her mother, that she seems to be projecting some of her own bad experiences with men. Just as they were about to leave, the young man asked to talk to me privately. The girl waited in my front yard.

"Rabbi," he said. "I lied to you. I have had a homosexual experience. When I was fifteen, a boy in the neighborhood and I went to bed together."

"Have you had any homosexual relations since then?"

"No."

"Well, I wouldn't worry very much about it then," I said. "It's very common for adolescent boys to play around this way. It's natural. You were in a period when you were forming your heterosexuality."

"Well," he asked, "do you think I should tell her?"

"That's up to you," I said.

He told her.

They were out in the front yard, and as I watched from my window, I could see she was growing very upset. They came back in.

"Don't be so upset," I told her. "What he did is not uncommon. Most boys have this kind of experience when they're young."

"Well," she said, "it simply reinforces what my mother has said all along. My mother was right."

August 4

The mother called me this morning to thank me. The girl moved out of her boy friend's apartment last night, went home and told everything.

"You have nothing to thank me for," I said. "I would have liked to see them stay together."

"What?"

"The boy is no homosexual," I said. "But, if anything, this experience could make him one."

I spent most of the day taking phone calls and taking care of Judith. We sat outside by the pool for a few hours, and she seemed to be feeling slightly better, but not much. It depresses me that I cannot help her. Her problems are so complex that often I cannot tell how she is going to react to anything. She asks me to make up her mind for her on nearly every matter, and while I don't want her to feel abandoned, I don't want her to feel that I have to think for her. This afternoon, she asked me, for instance, whether she should put on her bathing suit.

"If you want to, honey."

"But what do you think? Should I?"

"I think you should do it if you want to, and not do it if you don't want to."

"I don't know whether I want to or not."

"But you should be the one who decides."

"But whether I do it or not depends on what you want me to do."

It is an endless entanglement; she and I are both trapped in our ambivalences. I want to help her and I don't want to hurt her at the same time. She feels she needs to please me and is uncertain whether in pleasing herself, she would please me.

And we get nowhere.

August 5

I spent most of the day preparing for the Jewish-Christian Institute to be held at Grailville, Ohio, next week. Judith's psychiatrist has given her permission to come with me; he is convinced that her illness can be treated outside the hospital. Since our mutual unspoken fear has been that she would have to be hospitalized, she was delighted by the doctor's diagnosis. So was I.

I made plans for both of us to fly to Charleston with Sally. We'll leave Sally there, fly to Grailville, then, after the Institute, spend a few days with my in-laws. Getting away may be just what Judith needs.

August 6

Some of the more progressive members of the congregation and I have worked out a series of innovations for our services, and tonight I presented our proposals to the worship committee, the guardians of the status quo.

I suggested, among other things, that we replace the sermon with discussions. I would miss my sermons, even if no one else would—sometimes I think I'm the only one who gets my message —but, still, I feel a service should be a happening, not a conventional theatrical production. A service should be a gathering where people can get up and say anything about anything for any reason. The ultimate religious experience is communication. Prayer is supposed to be communication, between people and between people and God. If you can't communicate with people, how can you communicate with God?

I also recommended that we hold periodic multi-media services, using music, film, and anything else available to us. Multi-media is modern communication, and if prayer is to be meaningful to us, we must bring it into the twentieth century.

Another suggestion was that we make our holidays more joyous, instituting, for instance, a singing and dancing procession on such occasions as Simchas Torah.

"Very good idea," said one of the older committee members, "except let me ask you one thing."

"Yes?"

"Who is going to choreograph the procession? Should we put a dance teacher on the temple staff?"

"Rabbi," one older woman said, as if I were a child and she were telling me something for the tenth time, "when I come to services, I want to pray. That's what I pay my temple dues for and that's what I want."

"She's right," said an ally. "I like it just the way it is. I don't need any change."

"You see, Rabbi," somebody else said, "I came to religion late. It makes me feel good and I don't want to change it."

I didn't expect them to react any differently. After a couple of years of sparring with them, I know the routine: I make my proposals; they demur; I press; they suggest compromises.

Tonight, for example, although they couldn't accept a service without sermons, they agreed to have the Torah portion read aloud in Hebrew and English every several weeks to be followed by a congregational discussion. This is, at least, a start and, hopefully, it will loosen them up to go even further.

They, of course, also rejected the concept of the multi-media service as a *service*, but after much discussion I convinced them that they would not be betraying their role as protectors of the past if they accepted it instead as a special event. They agreed to a multi-media special event.

The proposal for more joyous holidays?

"I'll do the choreography," I said.

They laughed.

They are really very decent people. They just have to be coddled.

After the meeting, I conducted a simple conversion ceremony in my home for the young lady whose in-laws sent her to me last spring and asked that I produce an instant Jew. In the past several months, I have been working with the girl—I gave her readings more basic than Martin Buber, whom she felt she could not understand—and she has developed, I believe, a meaningful commitment to Judaism.

In the ceremony, I asked her the standard questions—Do you give up your former faith? Do you identify yourself with the people of Israel?—and she gave the standard answers. I pronounced her Jewish. Usually, when I allow myself to think about it, I realize how silly this ritual is, but tonight I felt the ceremony had substance. The young lady seemed deeply moved. She had overcome her in-laws' dominance. She wasn't doing this for them. She was doing it for herself.

August 7

Today we flew to Charleston, where we will leave Sally while we attend the Institute at Grailville. Judith is feeling much better, and I hope that this vacation will allow her to work things out in her mind.

August 8

My in-laws live in a section of Charleston known as the Battery, an enclave of elegant old mansions. Their home, facing a park which fronts on the Atlantic Ocean, is five stories tall. The ground floor, which was formerly the slave quarters, has been converted into twenty efficiency apartments. On the first floor is a double drawing room, a dining room, a kitchen, a ballroom—all set off from a lovely center hall which is furnished with my father-in-law's collection of African masks, antiques, and primitive art. My in-laws live on the second floor, where there are three suites, a large study, a master bedroom, an office, and a dressing room. We are staying in one of the suites on this floor. Porches completely circle the first and second floors of the house. On the third floor are two more suites; the fourth floor is now used for storage, although it was originally a play area for the children. The grounds, well tended and dotted with a number of fountains, are enclosed by a beautiful wrought-iron gate and guarded by two sculptured lions.

Charleston, despite its charm and beauty, is a very decadent city. It is struggling to preserve a way of life that should have vanished with the Civil War. With great emphasis on family background, the whole place smacks of elitism. As my father-in-law said today, Charleston has just joined America. He was referring to the recent hospital workers' strike, a cause célèbre for the blacks and white liberals which even induced Al Lowenstein to come down here to investigate.

For the longest time I really loved this city, but now I am very ambivalent about it. I love its quiet, rustic beauty, its gracious style, but I detest how it stands so squarely in the way of a new life, a life of justice, for the poor black people.

Dinner was served to us tonight by black maids, in a dining area which glittered from all the old family silver.

It ruined my appetite. Throughout the meal, I thought back to the old black woman who had worked as a maid for my mother for fifteen years. She was a wonderfully humane woman who befriended me and looked after me and cared for me. I really loved her.

Unfortunately, she had all kinds of problems. She lived in a terrible slum; her many husbands, some of whom were alcoholics, rarely worked. She was often penniless. Yet, whenever my mother needed her, whatever her situation was, she would always be there. Then one day she had a stroke and died.

My mother never even went to her funeral.

August 9

Judith spent most of today with her mother and I with my memories.

I recalled our wedding here. It was the social event of the season. Judith, as a member of a leading family, was marrying not only a rabbi, but a Marine captain. The ceremony was performed by two rabbis. I was very impressed with the first rabbi's technique. He had memorized the entire wedding service, and said it, rather than read it, something I am still unable to do. The second rabbi gave a sort of inaugural address, going on at great length about how a rabbi's life was different, how a rabbi's wife was different, how wonderful I was, how wonderful Judith was. Finally, I had to gesture to him: cut it. Enough is enough.

The ceremony was not entirely as I would have liked it. I had made a few suggestions: first, that since a large number of non-Jews would be attending, we write up a program so they could follow along. My mother-in-law vetoed that. Second, caught up as I was in those days in the splendor of the ambience, I suggested that we ride from the temple to the house in an open horse-drawn carriage. My mother-in-law vetoed that, too.

Finally, since I would be attending the ceremony in my uniform, and since a large number of Marines would be attending, I proposed that we have an honor guard of Marines crossing their swords as we left the chapel. My mother-in-law also vetoed that. It was her show.

What a show! The reception was catered at the Tobiases' home, in the ballroom, and more than 500 people, including many Marine officers in full-dress uniform, attended. As is the style in Charleston, there was more to drink than to eat.

I find the whole recollection somewhat embarrassing.

August 10

We left Sally in Charleston and flew to Cincinnati this morning for the conference at Grailville. It was the first time we had ever been separated from Sally, but both of us, especially Judith, needed the break.

Grailville is a complex of old buildings on what used to be a farm not far from Cincinnati. The Grail, a group of secular nuns, founded in Holland, has gained a reputation as an open, experimental, avant-garde group within the Catholic Church. Most Grail nuns are married, none wear habits, and all work at secular pursuits. For the most part, they are liberal and intellectually concerned Catholics.

Grailville is the sort of place where Jews and Christians may study each other's heritage without either group being polemical or defensive. This is our second annual conference here, and approximately twenty-five people, most of them Grail nuns, are attending.

As general chairman of the institute, I formally opened the session this evening. I said what I felt: that Jews and Christians have never really communicated. On the one hand, the church has resisted any dialogue, and on the other hand, Jews tend to be defensive and tell Christians what they want to hear: "We're all the same." In my talk, I laid the groundwork for my theory of the Judaization of Christianity, which, as it was at Marymount, will be the subject of my lectures here.

Since the institute is financially sponsored by the American Jewish Congress, the speaker who followed me was an AJC representative making a pitch for the AJC. I guess that's the price you pay for AJC auspices.

August 13

During a break in the institute today, I went up to Cincinnati and visited my old school, Hebrew Union College. I don't really know why I wanted to see the place; I didn't enjoy my years there.

I went to Hebrew Union almost by accident. When I decided to become a rabbi, during my senior year at Cornell, I knew no one who had ever applied to rabbinical school. I assumed that I would have no trouble getting in, that my Cornell degree would awe any admission board. I had a very large view of myself, and since I had decided to be a rabbi, I assumed that was enough. Who would stand in my way?

I casually filled out my applications—if I made mistakes, I just crossed them out with red pencil; I didn't bother retyping—and then interviewed the various rabbinical schools, instead of allowing them to interview me.

First, I went to the Jewish Theological Seminary, a training ground for Conservative Judaism. An admissions officer, a round little man, told me that as a student I would have to sign a pledge to observe the rules of *Kashrut,* the kosher laws, but that I needn't take the pledge too seriously. "Signing the pledge is the important thing," he said. "What you do afterward is your own business."

I gave up on the Jewish Theological Seminary. I felt Judaism needed me more than I needed them.

Once I made up my mind I wanted to be a Reform rabbi, I was faced by a monopoly: only Hebrew Union College manufactured Reform rabbis. My choice was merely between its New York branch and its Cincinnati branch. When I applied, the admissions board summoned me to Cincinnati for an interview. Since, at Cornell, I was much closer to Manhattan than Ohio, I wrote back and told them that if they wanted the pleasure of an interview with me, it would have to be in New York.

The interview was held in New York. I don't remember the details, except that no one asked me to sign a pledge to observe *Kashrut,* and one of my interviewers, impressed by my white bucks, chinos, and knit tie, called me "Jack Armstrong, the All-American Boy."

I was quickly admitted, and then had to choose my branch. The New York branch struck me as a subway school; I decided I could get a more intensive Jewish education in Cincinnati.

I found the school a bore. With only a few exceptions, the teaching was third-rate, and the intellects second-rate, and, faced with no challenge, I responded poorly. I got into academic difficulty immediately. My first six months, I had to take a course in Hebrew grammar with a Dr. Epstein, a man who seemed to consider proper Hebrew conjugation at least one level holier than Godliness. He terrified me. He reduced me to a memorizing mummy. As a result, I developed a block about the Hebrew language that affected me all through rabbinical school.

I failed a course in Talmud—the study of the laws depended heavily on a working knowledge of the Aramaic dialect of Hebrew—the first time I'd ever flunked any academic course. I was tempted many times to give up, to leave Cincinnati and my rabbinical ambitions behind, but, somehow, I struggled through. I was ordained, given my trade-school diploma.

Perhaps it was because I never quite knew why I was there that I could never quite get up and leave.

August 16

The Grailville Institute ended today—my lecture on the Judaization of Christianity was very well received—and Judith is remarkably improved. She looks better, feels better, and is acting better than at any time since her breakdown in May. As a result, I am feeling wonderful myself.

This was just what she needed, a week away from it all—Sally, the house, the role of the Rabbi's Wife. I hope that, with the new strength she has found here, her readjustment will be comfortable.

August 17

Judith and I flew back to Charleston today, and when we arrived, at nine in the evening, Sally ran up to me and said in a big, loud voice, "Daddy." It made me feel good. She's a very bright, alive, and active child, and Judith and I both missed her.

We drove back to my in-laws' mansion, ate dinner and fell asleep, exhausted.

August 18

The Tobiases are very unusual people. My father-in-law is an expert amateur historian who has written numerous articles on

Jewish history, two of which were recently chosen for the anniversary edition of the American Jewish Historical Society publication. He once worked for the *New Yorker* and then, until he retired five years ago, he was in the public-relations business in Charleston, His health, recently, has not been very good.

My mother-in-law was born into an aristocratic Georgia family distantly related to Woodrow Wilson. She converted to Judaism when she married my father-in-law.

The Tobiases are part of a neo-aristocracy here. Much in their home reinforces that impression: expensive antiques, works of art, silver goblets, fine china, servants, the decorum, the whole bit. It was in this setting that Judith grew up, and recently I have begun to wonder if part of her problem does not stem from the fact that she is a trained aristocrat living in a society which no longer recognizes aristocracy.

At dinner this evening, this must have been on my mind, because the conversation turned to raising children.

"We believe in placing great emphasis on discipline," my mother-in-law said.

"I don't," I said. "Too much discipline stifles children. The emphasis should be on fulfillment of potential. A child is like a flower, and the role of its parents should be to help it unfold."

The conversation never got angry, but we each knew that what we were saying related to Judith's problems. For the first time, I sensed they may feel a tinge of guilt.

After dinner, my father-in-law and I went for a walk. He spoke of his deep love for Charleston, and his deep appreciation for proportion and beauty. We also talked about the archives he started in his temple, his project to restore a Jewish cemetery in Charleston where Jews who died in the Revolutionary War were buried, and about a Jewish historical mural he has commissioned.

August 19

I got a long-distance call from Temple Sinai this morning. There is a new crisis with the cantor, and I am supposed to return to help solve it. I was given the background on the phone.

The cantor is on vacation this month, but he was asked, a week ago, to officiate at a bar mitzvah that will fall on the *fifth* Saturday of August. He flatly refused. "Don't bother me," he told them. "I'm on vacation."

Since this is an unusual circumstance, the officers of the congregation asked him to work the day of the bar mitzvah and promised him a week off later. He wouldn't even discuss it.

The incident prompted him to write a letter to the chairman of the worship committee, in which he charged that my wife, Judith, was not really sick, that I had fabricated the whole thing in order to take an extra week's vacation. He said I had done this only to embarrass him, because he doesn't get such long vacations. Furthermore, he said, that in the little vacation he does get, the congregation annoys him with phone calls such as the one he got last week.

The members of the temple board then sent him a telegram warning him that if he didn't promise to show up for the bar mitzvah, he would be asked to appear before the executive committee. He didn't answer. Then they sent him a registered letter, in which they informed him that the executive committee would be meeting to discuss his future, and that his attendance was requested. He didn't show up. Then, the executive committee decided to send him another telegram, this time warning him if he didn't show up for the bar mitzvah he would be fired. He has not yet answered.

From the way I heard the story, it sounds as if they are getting ready to fire him. But I don't believe it. The cantor has always had a fantastic ability to survive. At the moment, anyway, he knows he is operating from a position of strength. With the High Holy Days only a few weeks off, he knows that the congregation needs him too badly to fire him now.

In a way, I felt flattered that they called me and told me they needed me to help them through this. I'm also annoyed at what the cantor said about me feigning Judith's illness, but I've always known him to be considerably less than tactful.

We packed tonight and prepared to cut our rest short and leave for home tomorrow.

August 20

On our flight to New York today, we were delayed taking off, we were delayed landing, the baggage was delayed and our transportation from the airport was delayed.

I sensed that Judith was already beginning to feel strained.

August 21

This morning I talked with Judith at length, because I felt that getting away had done her a great deal of good, and I'm afraid that now, in coming home, it will all be lost.

By dinner time, she was in as bad a condition as ever. She

said she felt she could relate to nothing. Her eyes had grown vacant, and she seemed to wander about dazed.

We went to see her psychiatrist this evening. He told her she might have to go to the hospital, which only made matters worse. He said to me that she had reached the point where he didn't think he could help her anymore, and a more intensive form of therapy would be required.

After we left the doctor, we came home.

Then, even though I don't believe in miracles, one occurred.

Judith perked up, as if nothing had happened, and within the hour she was cleaning the kitchen, seeming even better than she was in Charleston, as good, in fact, as she was last spring before she got sick at all.

At this moment, she is in her little office figuring out the checkbook. She seems to have snapped out of this thing miraculously.

There are a lot of things which happen outside nature, a lot we don't and shouldn't understand. As human beings, we operate outside the so-called laws of science. Maybe by a miracle, Judith has been cured.

August 22

It all fell apart today.

Judith could not operate. At dinner, she got up from the table, went to lie down, and has not functioned since. She is just lying there. Awake.

When I went into the bedroom to talk to her earlier, she remained silent. She said only one sentence: "Martin, I just don't want to be around anymore."

I know now that I have to face it: she is seriously ill. No miracle is going to occur. She must be cured before she harms herself.

I called her psychiatrist, and told him what she said.

"Well, what do *you* think, Rabbi?" he asked. That's his style. Mister Cool. Always playing the damn game. This whole psychiatric thing is a way of life in itself, an internal society of cool professionals who spend their time verifying each other. They may help people, but at this moment they make me sick.

"You're the doctor," I said. "What do *you* think?"

He said he would see her in the morning.

Later in the evening, I left Judith with my mother and went to conduct services. I think I read the service with a degree of conviction I haven't felt in a long time. I can't believe that prayers will make Judith well again, but as communication to a greater dimension, at least they are therapeutic for me. I prayed very hard tonight.

August 23

Judith saw the doctor briefly today. "She is very ill," he said. "I can no longer handle her. She will have to go to the hospital."

I called University Hospital in Brooklyn to have her admitted. The mechanics of mental health in our society demand that one must first get seriously ill and then wait while the bureaucracy clears the way for treatment. I couldn't get an appointment with a doctor at the hospital until three days from now.

Meanwhile, Judith is just getting worse and worse, more erratic in her behavor, more unsure of herself, more phlegmatic, more irrational. She can't cope with anything. My mother had to come out to take care of the house.

What I mistook for a miracle the other night was just one up in a series of ups and downs. Sometimes for a brief moment, Judith is seemingly able to relate, and then, moments later, she is as disassociated as ever.

August 24

Even though I came home to help the congregation through its crisis with the cantor, I have not had a spare moment to meet with anybody on the matter. Today Bob Mandel called and told me the cantor has not yet answered the last telegram, the one threatening to fire him if he doesn't show up next Saturday for the bar mitzvah.

I left the house only once all day—to co-officiate with a priest at a marriage between a young lady in my congregation and a Catholic.

After the wedding, I came home, where my mother has more or less taken over. My mother has been a problem for Judith and a problem for me, but whenever we need her, she is always here. Now she's cooking, cleaning, taking care of Sally and managing the household. Judith is so drugged up on tranquilizers, she has been asleep most of the day. She knows that I am going to try and have her admitted to the hospital, and she is not objecting. She wants to be able to function again.

This crisis with Judith has finally made my mother much more sensitive to what is happening. My mother is a very strong-willed woman, and for months now I've tried to explain to her that she must be more gentle with Judith. "You don't like me and you have no respect for me," she would say.

"You don't understand, Mother," I would tell her. "I do love you and I do have respect for you, but I reserve the right in my house to have things done the way I want them, and you just can't come in here and take over."

"I'm sorry," she would say. "I'm an old lady. I can't change."

But in the past few days, she has been marvelous. I don't know what I would do without her here. She is really devoted to taking care of Sally, and through all this, she has been very decent and tender toward Judith.

August 25

Judith's appointment to see the doctor at the hospital is set for tomorrow. But today I had to go into the office. There has still been no word from the cantor, and they are now talking as if they are really getting ready to fire him. But that's his problem. Not mine.

I had to deal with another crisis today. I had encouraged the son of Audrey Brackman, the principal of our religious school, to help us edit our temple bulletin. Having had some experience with an underground newspaper, the first article he prepared for the bulletin was a statement on why he would not attend the High Holy Day services. Essentially, he called the temple a living hypocrisy. I wrote a small piece to run beside his in which I answered his charges, not exactly wholeheartedly.

Still, when Bob Mandel saw the boy's article, he felt it would be harmful to Mrs. Brackman if it were to run. I disagreed, but was in no mood for a major confrontation. I agreed to tone the article down.

Later in the day I got a call from Al Lowenstein's office, but I had my secretary say I wasn't in. I have been avoidng a number of commitments to the things that so infatuated me this past year. My only concern now is with Judith's health. I am unable to ward off a sense of guilt; perhaps if I had shown some concern for her health earlier this year, all of this would never have happened.

August 26

I drove Judith to University Hospital in Brooklyn early this afternoon for an appointment with a doctor. The doctor immediately recommended she be hospitalized. He told me to take her home and help her get packed and bring her back tomorrow to check in.

When we arrived home, my mother had dinner prepared for us. She looked utterly exhuasted. Sally is unbelievably active; if I had to take care of her all day, I'd probably be going to the hospital, too. There is no way to stop the child. Tonight I found myself changing her diapers; I guess I'll be making quite a few adjustments now. I also spent some time this evening arranging to hire a housekeeper.

Judith didn't eat dinner. Almost as soon as we got home from the hospital, she went to sleep. The past few days, if she has not been sleeping, she has been in a sleepy state. It's very difficult when you see someone you know so well, who has been so full of life, fall into a state like this. She is so listless it is virtually impossible to move her

My mother helped me pack for Judith. It was such an awful feeling, packing her clothes to take her to the hospital and leave her there. I can't believe this is happening. I feel so strange, so frightened for her.

I hope to God she can get well soon.

August 27

This morning Judith was all but lifeless. Even getting her dressed was a problem. As we left the house, my mother looked at her and said, "She is walking out of here like a stone."

It was so odd. She was sick, and I was driving her to the hospital, all so matter-of-factly, as if we were off to the supermarket. For most of the hour-long trip, she remained silent. I kept thinkng: What could I have done to prevent this? I kept tormenting myself.

When we arrived at the hospital, two nurses in street clothes came down from the psychiatric ward and escorted Judith to her room. I was not allowed to go with her. Instead, they sent me to the finance department, where I was told that it will cost $100 a day to keep Judith here. The insurance will cover most of this for the first thirty days, but if she has to be here longer, we could be devastated financially.

Afterward, when I went upstairs to help Judith get settled in her room, another patient strolled in and asked Judith what she planned to do for lunch.

"Oh," Judith said, "I'm going to order room service."

"Don't be frightened," the patient said to her. "Everybody is a little scared when they first come here. Why don't you come down and have lunch with us?"

I broke down completely. For the first time in a long time, I cried. I couldn't help myself. I went out into the hallway and cried.

Judith looked so scared I couldn't bear it. I left.

I spent the afternoon with Sally. She was cranky, and I believe it's because, even though she is quite young, she realizes something is missing.

In the evening, I drove back to the hospital, but Judith was already asleep.

August 28

I woke up gloomy. For the first time since we've lived in this house, Judith was not beside me. She is in a psychiatric ward, I thought to myself. Judith is in a psychiatric ward. I examined the import of these words. Is this really happening? Is my wife really in a mental institution?

It was a depressing way to wake up, and the depression stayed with me all day long. If I functioned, I did so automatically, because my mind seemed to be obsessed every minute with reliving, detail by detail, the events of yesterday.

In the morning, even though I went to the wrong train station at the wrong time to meet her, the housekeeper arrived. After that, I went to the office, where I had to go over some details for the new temple bulletin. But I couldn't get involved.

At noon, I drove to the hospital. But the nurse told me that Judith did not want to see me. She wanted to be left alone.

"Why?" I asked. "What have I done?"

"It's not you," the nurse said. "This is just a symptom of her illness."

The nurse sent me to talk to Judith's doctor.

"Judith is very angry, Rabbi." the doctor told me, "because she has always repressed her anger. She has never developed a capacity to be negative, and therefore she is incapable of expressing her negative feelings. She was so angry yesterday that she couldn't even sit through my entire interview. She probably doesn't want to see you today because she is angry and she doesn't know how to deal with her anger in front of you."

"But is she angry *at* me?" I asked.

"I don't know," he said. "Yet."

For the next two hours he asked me a lot of questions, some of them very probing, and I answered as honestly as I could. When it was over, I realized that he had helped me to pull some of the pieces together.

I think I now see that what happened to Judith was inevitable. She was the victim of circumstances, and bad luck.

When we lived in Wheeling, everything was fine. I, of course, was always aware of her two previous breakdowns, but I believed that she was fully recovered. I had friends. She had friends. We had friends. She had her *own* role in the community, not only that of the rabbi's wife. She had people she could talk to. She felt she belonged. She was involved. I was home more often. When I wasn't, I was at work in the community, and she was part of that community. My activities outside the house were highly visible to her. There was never any problem with my mother. She was a couple of hundred miles away, and since my father was sick and she had to take care of him, her visits were infrequent.

Then came the offer from Temple Sinai. The big leagues. We discussed it. We felt it was time for us to move on. Judith encouraged me to take the offer. I did.

In the space of two months, we moved to Woodmere, we had a baby and my father died. Suddenly, Judith, naturally shy, tied down by the new baby, a newcomer to a community that vould not encourage easy friendships, found herself without a life of her own. To complicate matters, my mother, much closer to us geographically, compensating for the loss of my father, became a regular visitor. And, gradually, Sally emerged from infancy into a personality, an active personality, sometimes difficult to deal with. All these factors—Judith's new loneliness, my mother's frequent inspection tours, Sally's demands—coincided, at least in Judith's mind, with an increase in my outside activities. She needed me more than ever, and I gave her less support.

Perhaps worst of all, I was not attuned to the way she was expressing her feelings, the quiet hints she gave off, the muted messages she sent. I was too involved in my activities in the community, and now the community was Metropolitan New York, and Judith was not really a part of it.

Once I realized what was happening last spring, I tried everything I knew to pull her out of it, but in retrospect, I now realize that the path she traveled all along led only in this direction. Here. To the hospital. There were good times this summer, and there were times when it seemed as if there would be movement, but I now see that every step was backwards. The larger problem was only further repressed, not solved.

In the end, she wanted to come here to the hospital, and the doctor now tells me that this is a good sign. She realizes she is very sick and she wants to be cured. I hope so. I hope this thing can be reversed.

The doctor told me the method of treatment for her will be a therapeutic community in which Judith and other patients will learn to help one another, and at the same time be encouraged to experiment with forms of behavior new to them. Then, from the strength she develops in this therapeutic community, she will be able to reenter her own community, having at least proved to herself that she can triumph over her own repressions.

He didn't say it, but what this really means, I suppose, is that she will be encouraged to break up her personality in order to be able to build it all over again in a manner more natural to her instincts.

I find this very frightening, but I realize it is our only chance.

August 29

Now that the housekeeper is tending to the house and Sally, my mother was able to go home today.

Before Judith went into the hospital, I contracted with a fellow to complete the patio around our pool. He showed up today, but he didn't have enough flagstone. I trooped over to a neighbor's house where I had seen some extra flagstone in the yard, and asked if we could borrow a few.

The neighbors said yes and asked me, casually, how things were. I told them my wife was in the hospital.

They seemed genuinely concerned. They invited me to their yacht club to go sailing Saturday afternoon. I really appreciated the invitation, because it will give me an opportunity to relax. Nobody else has given a damn, has shown any concern at all. Everybody floats in their own orbit in this community, and if their orbit happens to cross your orbit and nobody would be greatly inconvenienced, they are anxious to help. The people here are so damn brutal.

When I visited Judith in the hospital this afternoon, she appeared to be slightly improved. At least, she would talk to me. I have a feeling that this is because of the other patients: they all seemed to be concerned with one another. What irony! These people, the people the society calls sick, are the ones who are able to form what really constitutes a community of concern.

As I was getting ready to leave the hospital, a meeting of

the therapeutic community was announced. Judith shoved me away. She was anxious to go to the meeting.

She seems to have found some relation to this therapeutic community, and I am not a part of it. I guess I am not part of it because I am part of the problem.

There was much speculation tonight at services as to whether the cantor would show up tomorrow.

August 30

The cantor didn't show up this morning. The president didn't expect him to. We had a substitute cantor waiting in the wings, and the bar mitzvah went on unhindered. On Monday, the temple board will meet to decide whether to fire the cantor.

In the afternoon, I went to the yacht club with my neighbors, then drove to the hospital to see Judith.

She was more animated than I'd seen her in a few weeks. She has started to complain. The hospital staff, she says, does not know what it is doing. She says her therapy is not structured enough. They have done no good for her, she insists. I noted that as we walked down the hallways in the hospital, whenever we would encounter a group of patients, she would steer me away. "I'm still afraid of people," she said.

The doctors say her complaints are a good sign, but I am beginning to suspect that the doctors say everything is a good sign.

The day left me very confused.

August 31

When I visited Judith in the hospital this afternoon, she had just finished a painting, and was getting ready to cook lunch for some other patients. I was delighted.

The president called me and said he is in favor of firing the cantor immediately, and using a substitute cantor for the High Holy Days. He asked me what I thought.

"I don't care," I said.

September 1

The cantor resigned this morning.

He called Audrey Brackman, the educational director, and told her, "I've had it. I can't fight anymore."

Apparently, someone had tipped him off about tonight's meeting, and he decided to quit before he was fired.

I find myself ambivalent about his resignation. I do think, to a degree, that he was a genuinely put-upon person, that he did suffer as a result of his relationship with the congregation. On the other hand, he was a pain in the neck. Every six weeks, there was something on his mind for which I or the congregation was always to blame.

For a long time, I was his ally, because, like him, I was an employee of the congregation and I knew what happened to him might someday happen to me. Therefore, we had to stick together. But he was such a difficult man to deal with. As he himself said, he had no interest in institutional Judaism and he couldn't have cared less about Temple Sinai. And, as he had made known on more than one occasion, he had little regard for me.

I tried to reach out and communicate with him. A few times, I felt that I was succeeding. But then with this last incident, in which he tried to undo me, my mercy ended. *Why me?* I asked myself. *Why did he attack me?* The only reason I could imagine was that somehow he had made me the symbol of his real or imagined oppression. I was younger than he, and I made more money. He blamed me for his own shortcomings.

An interview with another cantor was quickly arranged for tonight's meeting. We all asked the man some very sharp questions about his convictions toward Judaism and his feelings on the role of the cantor. After more than a decade and a half with a cantor who cared nothing for Judaism and who took a strictly pray-for-pay attitude, we intend to be very selective in choosing a replacement. We asked the man if he would care to "try out." He said he would.

At the hospital today, Judith showed me two paintings she had finished. She seemed to be adjusting better to life there, or, at least, complaining less.

I am finding my own adjustment very difficult. I don't like life with a housekeeper.

September 2

I saw some neighbors on the street this morning, and they looked at me very solemnly. "If there is anything we can do," they said, "let us know."

I assume they have heard about Judith. It's funny how people skirt the nature of her problem. They seem afraid even to mention mental illness.

A few days ago, I decided to enroll Sally in nursery school at Temple Israel, because Temple Sinai doesn't have a nursery school and a teacher there is the wife of a friend of mine. I never considered the cost, but somebody affiliated with the school suggested to me that, as a rabbi, I shouldn't have to pay. I should get a courtesy. Since I've given talks at Temple Israel many times without any fee, I thought this was a good idea. I dropped the hint in a few places that I would not like to have to pay for Sally's nursery school.

This morning their religious-school director came to see me in person. He said he was pleased to inform me that the board of directors or the nursery-school committee or something like that has decided to permit Sally to enroll in the school at half price.

"It's very nice of you," I said, "to give it to me wholesale."

Later in the day, I went to Brooklyn to see Judith, and had a nice, relaxed conversation. She seemed genuinely sad to see me leave, but she said good-bye on a rather strange note.

"If you have something better to do," she said, "don't bother to come here."

She must be testing me.

September 3

I went to the hospital this morning, and when I returned to my office, I discovered I'd forgotten an appointment with a gentleman who had come out to see me from New York. He had already returned to the city. I felt awful. As a rule, I like to live chaotically, but somehow I just have to develop a sense of order so that people who rely on me won't be inconvenienced like this. Things have gotton so much worse since Judith has been in the hospital; I always relied on her to keep me organized.

I had lunch with the temple's accountant, who told me the temple is in serious financial difficulty. We have lost thirty families this year, while signing up only ten new ones. The lost families quit because they disapproved of me or because they did not care to contribute to the building fund or because the services they required—the bar mitzvah, the confirmation, the wedding—had been rendered. New membership is at a standstill because anyone who joins the temple this year is asked to pay $350 for the new building, plus the annual dues of $250. This is quite a steep tariff for a synagogue now operating out of a Masonic Temple.

In the evening, the cantor issue dominated a meeting of the worship committee. Much was said about how he insulted me by charging that my wife's illness was a hoax to get me more vacation time. From the way people spoke, this seemed to be the final reason for firing him. I didn't say anything. I just listened. The tone of the discussion was remarkable. Here was a man who, in spite of everything else, had week in and week out served the temple for seventeen years, and nobody really seemed to care about him. Everything said about him was deprecating. Nobody raised a whisper of compassion, including me.

After the meeting, I met privately with Bob Mandel. He said that the executive committee had worked out my proposed new contract and we discussed the terms. I will get an immediate raise of $2,000 (to $18,000) and an additional raise of $750 a year, which will come partly in a housing allowance and partly in salary. In light of what the accountant told me at lunch, I figured that this was as generous as they could be. The contract will run for three years, not five. Since Mandel convinced me that a longer contract might present economic problems and bind me beyond my will, I accepted this provision. Also, as I examine my motives for asking for the five-year contract, I find them to be more a measure of my insecurity than anything else. So, in this sense, it would be an embarrassing point to haggle over. As for my request to have a provision written into the contract which specified that I had a right to resign if the membership grew too large, Mandel talked me out of that, too. This is not a matter for the contract. I had made my point, and they are on notice that this is my intention.

I asked Mandel for only two changes: one, that it be specified that I am allowed to be absent from the congregation a number of weeks each year for professional purposes; two, that I have the right to secure other employment, such as teaching. Since I already exercise both these prerogatives anyway, he readily agreed to them. Later this month the board of trustees will meet and vote on the contract.

"Now that this is all over," Mandel said, "I'd like to ask one thing of you. There is something I would like you to stress in the coming year."

"And what is that?" I asked.

"Don't be permissive with the kids," he said. "Tell them what is right and tell them what is wrong. Give them clear moral direction."

September 4

Today was the housekeeper's day off and chaos reigned in the house. Even though my mother came out to help, Sally exhausted her to the point where she gave up trying to handle the child. I had to arrange for a number of people in the community to take care of her; I literally passed her from hand to hand throughout the day.

In the afternoon, I spent a few frustrating hours with Judith's doctor, who told me that Judith has made some sort of breakthrough in the therapy, but he wouldn't give me the details or allow me to see her today. He would only tell me that because of the so-called breakthrough, Judith was very upset and was receiving special attention from a psychiatric social worker.

He didn't say so, but I guess they consider me a very important part of her problem, or else they wouldn't keep the details from me.

We talked at length about my relationship with Judith, and a few interesting things came out in the discussion.

He pointed out, as I knew, that Judith was constantly looking after me, picking up things I dropped, finding things I lost, remembering things I forgot. She never minded this role, however, because it gave her a sense of being needed. But when Sally started to become very difficult to take care of, Judith couldn't properly look after me. Cooking, worrying about the house, worrying about Sally and worrying about where I left my glasses became too much for her to handle. This upset her. It destroyed her sense of order, and therefore made her feel that she was failing me. She knew I needed her, but she felt she couldn't furnish what I needed anymore. Yet she would never complain. It was not her nature to complain. She took it all inside, and, in part, this is what caused her breakdown, or so the doctor says, and it appears very logical to me.

He brought up another point I had not considered. I treated Judith like a child. I always protected her, looked out for her and watched over her. Therefore, she had grown extremely dependent on me. On the other hand, there were also times I encouraged her to be independent; I rejected certain roles she wanted me to play. This confused her. For instance, she would always ask me what she should wear, because she wanted to dress to please me. "Those are decisions you have to make for yourself," I would tell her. I never realized the condescension in that remark.

I picked Sally up on my way home from the hospital, my mother fed her, and we put her to sleep. She demands so much attention it is virtually impossible to get anything done when she is around. One of the decisions I've made is that when Judith returns home, Sally will eat dinner by herself.

Tonight I polled the new confirmation class on a hypothetical question: If it were a prerequisite to give up Judaism in order to get into a good college, would you give it up?

Thirteen of the fourteen said they would.

I think that's a good measure of the future of the Jewish religion.

September 5

Since Judith's illness, my days have fallen into a routine. In the morning, I go to the office and take care of things that have to be done. Then I usually order out for a sandwich and eat lunch with the office staff. At around two o'clock, I drive to the hospital, spend a few hours with Judith, then drive home and have dinner with Sally. I'm doing a great deal to take care of Sally. I change her diapers, I train her and I put her to bed. I don't like her to be handled by the housekeeper, or even by my mother. It is the parents' responsibility to take care of the child. After she is asleep, I usually go out to a meeting.

Judith looked very depressed this afternoon.

"Martin," she asked, "how much is this hospital costing? It must be a fortune."

"That's not for you to worry about," I said. "All we care about is that you get well again."

"You know," she said, "we've had two major expenditures this year: the swimming pool and my hospitalization."

She really resents that pool. She never wanted it, and I talked her into it. I remember her words: "Go ahead, if you want it." I wish I hadn't.

She was very jittery all afternoon, almost out of control. I guess this is the "breakthrough" the doctor was talking about. I only hope that, after they tear her all apart, they can help her get back together again.

My sermon this evening dealt with the meaning of the High Holy Days, which start next week. I said they are a time when the rhythm of life changes, and each of us must look inward. They will be especially meaningful to me this year.

The organist, an elderly, frail bachelor and vegetarian, normally a very polite gentleman, was quite nervous tonight. He was so shook up he played off-key for most of the service. He had been very friendly with the cantor—the two were known in the congregation as the "Odd Couple"—and now with the cantor gone, he feels vulnerable. The cantor is a strong and domineering character, the organist is very submissive, and they always protected each other. I suspect that it was the organist who told the cantor he was about to be fired.

After the service, Bob Mandel explained to me further why he was anxious to fire the cantor. He sees me as the cantor's defender, and I think he feels guilty. He said he felt so strongly that he himself would have resigned if the cantor had not been fired.

September 6

Judith seems to be getting adjusted to the hospital, so adjusted, in fact, that she doesn't seem to be concerned with whether I come to visit her anymore. The doctors say she must learn to adjust to the group in the hospital before she can adjust to general society, and for this reason, I have become an unimportant part of her development.

Whenever I visit her, we talk about what is going on at home. Usually, she's very interested. This afternoon she wasn't.

Even though I know I have to see this as part of her sickness, it frustrates me.

Another crisis at Temple Sinai.

Audrey Brackman, our educational director, is in charge of scheduling bar mitzvahs. We try to give each young man a date as close to his thirteenth birthday as possible. Through a mix-up, she has slated two bar mitzvahs for the same day later this year, which is something we don't normally do.

Both families are upset, and since they have been putting Mrs. Brackman through hell, she is upset, too. She offered to do anything she could to accommodate them, but neither family would move. They both wanted their bar mitzvah on the day scheduled; neither wanted their son to share the pulpit with someone else. It was an absolute deadlock, so Mrs. Brackman asked me to negotiate a settlement.

I talked to both families. After much haggling, I finally persuaded one family to agree in principle to a double bar mitzvah. But they were rigid about the date. It had to be the one scheduled, because they had already rented a hall, hired a band, and made a commitment to a caterer. Then I went to the second family and explained to them the attitude of the first. They said they didn't care about the date, but they did not want a double bar mitzvah. Only one other date was available where the boy could have his bar mitzvah alone, and I offered it to them. But unfortunately that date fell in the middle of the Christmas vacation season. They rejected it.

"A lot of my friends will be in Florida on vacation," the mother said.

"Now look," I said, "who cares about your friends? Is this bar mitzvah for your son or for your friends?"

I embarrassed her. "All right, Rabbi," she said. "We'll have it on the Christmas date."

An hour later the phone rang. It was the mother of the second bar mitzvah boy. "Rabbi, I've been thinking about it," she said, "and I'm sorry, but we are going to have to have the bar mitzvah on the original date."

That was enough.

I called Mrs. Brackman and told her that both bar mitzvahs will remain on the day she scheduled them, and that if either family complained, she should tell them to go see King Solomon.

September 8

In the temple office, there are six of us working full time, including two secretaries. In working together over the years, we've all become involved with one another, sometimes to the point of having group therapy during lunch breaks. Each one brings his problems to the office, and the others sit and listen. Instead of the usual employee-employer relationships, there is a true feeling of participation, a community of concern.

A few weeks ago one of the secretaries left to go back to school. As a replacement, we hired a woman from Far Rockaway, a town across the city line in Queens County. She was a widow who was putting her son through college. I found her very pleasant. The rest of the staff did not. For one thing, because she was from Far Rockaway, they looked upon her as one step lower on the socio-economic ladder. She dressed a bit more flashy than the others, wore a little too much eye makeup and chewed gum. From the moment she set foot in the office, that was all I heard—how she chewed gum. Ladies of the Five Towns don't chew gum.

Today I came into the office and the other secretary smiled and said, "Rabbi, Estelle was fired."

"What do you mean, Estelle was fired?"

I learned that the ladies had gone to Bob Mandel and asked that she be removed.

The president gets deeply involved in some aspects of the temple, but stays aloof in others. In this instance, he didn't know much, or care much, about the situation. "Okay," he said. "We'll fire her."

Nobody consulted me, and without notice, Estelle was out of a job.

I called Mandel this afternoon and asked him why he fired her. "They told me she wasn't efficient," he said. "They said she misspelled words."

She had once misspelled the word "receipt" on a letter; as far as I know, that was the extent of her inefficiency. Her real crime, of course, was where she lived and how she dressed and the fact that she chewed gum.

I'm very upset about the whole thing.

It was a relatively good day for Judith. She seemed more alert than usual. She's taking charge of a dinner they are having at the hospital which will be prepared in a regular kitchen where patients are encouraged to cook their own meals. She seemed anxious to have me leave, because she wanted to get started. I am not used to her treating me with such casual aloofness, and it frightens me. But I have no choice: I have to trust the therapy.

In the evening, I met with the parents of the students in the confirmation class. I posed the same question to them that I had asked their children: If they had to give up Judaism in order to get their children into good colleges, would they give it up?

As I expected, they all waxed virtuous on the need for Jewish survival. So I pressed them as a group—and then individually—on why they felt Judaism should survive. Nobody had an answer. They had no reasons. They had never thought about it. They just accepted it. One parent grew irritated with me.

"I don't know, Rabbi," he said. "That's what you're paid for. *You* tell us why Judaism should survive."

September 9

In the evening I attended a very bruising meeting of the temple's board. The topic: the cantor.

The cantor had been in touch with a member of the board, complaining about a number of matters. This man, speaking as a mild advocate, listed the cantor's grievances to the board.

First, he said, the cantor felt he had been slighted last winter when he had not been asked to carry out the Torah at the concluding service in the old building. (The truth was that the cantor had refused to carry the Torah.) Also, the cantor now feels that he was not properly informed that he was expected to be back the last week of August to conduct a bar mitzvah. "He said he regarded the telegrams as peremptory in tone," the cantor's advocate said.

The president disputed both charges.

Then the discussion took a bizarre turn. Everybody became obsessed with the possibility that the cantor might try to set up some kind of demonstration to disrupt the High Holy Day services. The discussion rose to such hysteria that finally it was proposed the congregation hire a special police guard for the services.

"Now wait a minute," I protested. "I'm not conducting any services under armed guard. If the man shows up—and I doubt he will—then we will give him the hearing he wants."

"But what if he disrupts the services?" somebody asked.

"My God," I said, "the man has resigned. He's gone. Forget him already."

Finally they agreed that they would risk it and hold the regular High Holy Day services without police protection.

Then the man who started the whole discussion on the cantor took the floor once again. "Now I have my own complaint to make," he said. And believe it or not, his complaint was about an incident several months ago when I continued a discussion by a group of college students into the coffee-and-cake hour following the service.

"The bar mitzvah family pays for the coffee and cake and they should have a chance to serve it," he said rather harshly.

"Look," I said, "this is no time to be talking about what happened six months ago. The temple is in trouble. A temple, if it is to survive, needs people and in the last year we've lost nearly two families."

"What do you propose we do?" the president asked me.

"There's only one thing we can do," I said. "And that's to change the financial arrangements for new members. We cannot compel them to contribute $350 to the building fund."

There's nobody more self-righteous than a man who has paid his building-fund pledge. For the next hour, I had to listen to half a dozen "If-I-did-everybody-else-can" routines.

But finally, my proposal was brought to a vote, and by a small margin it was decided that the $350 levy on new members would be waived for the first year of their membership. The old Jewish instinct for survival prevailed again.

September 10

I have been asked on occasion: Who is the Rabbi's rabbi?

This morning it was the psychiatric social worker assigned to Judith's case. She called me to the hospital because she said she wanted to know more about my wife. As we talked, it became clear that what she really wanted was to know more about me.

"In curing Judith," she said, "one of the things that will have to be accomplished is for her to develop a new relationship with you. It's important that you understand her, and that we understand you. If we can understand you, we can help you deal with her."

I think she expected me to be reticent, but on the contrary, I was quite willing to discuss with her anything she wanted to know. In fact, I was anxious. There have been many things bothering me, and I wanted to talk about them. Her questions were helpful.

"Why did you marry your wife?" she asked.

"All of my life, love has been equated with achievement," I said. "I was highly pushed at all times to achieve, to do things for which I would receive awards of great love and affection from my mother. I see it today all over again with Sally. If Sally does something well for my mother, then she gets an award.

"What I loved from the start about Judith is that she demanded nothing. She was interested only in me, not my accomplishments. My fame and my ability were always secondary. What counted most was me as a human being. I needed that."

It was the first time I had ever articulated those words, and I felt very good in getting them out.

"The doctor says that you are very protective of Judith, that you treat her like a child," she said.

"Well," I said, "I've been thinking about that, and that's not entirely the case. If I were treating her like a child, I was not forcing her into this role because of my needs. She was forcing me into this role because of her needs."

"Even so," she said, "you treated her like a child."

"Well," I said, "I guess, to an extent, I did."

"Well then did you find that the advent of a real child strained your relationship?"

"How do you mean?"

"You were like a father with two children, and one wasn't getting enough attention."

After the talk with the social worker, I went to see Judith and found her in a jubilant mood.

They have given her permission to come home on a pass for Rosh Hashanah and Yom Kippur.

September 11

Until about a year ago, I had a deep fear of death. At night sometimes, I would wake up sweating profusely, my heart beating rapidly, filled with a terror of dying.

It was something I knew I had to work out. But only after I could accept the concept of time as a flow did I begin to feel a little more easy with the thought of my own death.

The state of unexistence no longer frightens me, because I now realize that man is only an expression of his moment, and when the moment fades, so must he. Whether I live or die is not important; it's what I do when I'm alive and what I contribute to the flow of time. Having worked this out in my mind, I have gained an inner peace, and it was in this mood I approached the High Holy Days, which began tonight with Rosh Hashanah. This year I am not going to pray for life, but for meaning. I am going to pray for a life that means something.

In my sermon tonight, I took a long look at man in his current moment. We are at a very important juncture in history, in between, in the words of one poet, the time of the gods who have fled and the gods who have yet to come. The search before us now is to find God in a new way, in new forms, in new meanings.

The great problem of our time is that man is alienated from himself, and from his society. Religion has yet to catch up with the new dimensions given him by science, intellect, and philosophy.

The time is now for a modern amalgamation, a great synthesis between the circumstances of life as it is being lived and religion. The wonder of religion in the past was that it bound man back to his universe and to himself. But now man stands alone with himself, a virtually self-contained computer who gets himself religiously serviced on Christmas Eve or Rosh Hashanah. He defers to old forms, but they have no substance to him in the way he lives his life.

The old gods are dead, gone. New ways to worship need to be discovered. Man must find a new vocabulary for his religious reality. He needs new understanding, new meanings, and new expressions of God. As it is, he is only running from himself, cloaking fears and self-doubts in hectic activity, afraid to plunge into himself to learn what he really feels, and resisting his own consciousness. And where through all of this, is God? God is just some venerated anachronism grandfather used to pray to.

And here I am, *Rabbi* Martin Siegel, keeping myself alive and earning a living (the phrase strikes me harshly) by preserving an institution in which God has grown meaningless. Yet I know that the life I've had given to me can't be satisfied by working furiously on the fringe of things. I want to be where people live.

I came here to create, not to cremate. But I know I am presiding over the last dying flame of a once great institution, offering tidbits of consolation to make the demise all the less painful. But nobody cares. Why do I bother?

If I were to die tomorrow, it could be said that my work was all useless—that Rabbi Martin Siegel turned over in the mausoleum where he worked and went to his death. He was a man who saw the past and saw the future, while he himself fell victim to a rapidly disintegrating present.

It is a very difficult self-inventory I find myself undertaking this Rosh Hashanah.

September 12

Services were held in a large auditorium, a borrowed hall at Woodmere Academy. The crowd was huge, and the spirit was festive: couples came holding hands, and everybody greeted each other with "Happy New Year." It struck me again that we are a very civilized people. We celebrate the New Year by coming to pray.

Judith, home on a pass, brought Sally to the children's service for the first time and sat her in the first row where I could watch her. After five minutes, she called out, "Daddy, that's long enough. Let's go home."

September 14

Every religion has an annual renewal festival, a time when people are supposed to think of who they are and where they are. It is also a time when they try to be sensitive to the things they have done wrong in the past year. The High Holy Day season which culminates in Yom Kippur, the day of atonement, is Judaism's season of renewal, and I always look upon it as a time to check in with God.

There were two people in the congregation whom, in the past year, I felt I had wronged, and today I visited both of them.

The first man is a senior civil servant in New York City, a very distinguished man who at one time was very active in the temple and served on the board and the worship committee. He is a traditionalist, and when I came here and began to upset some of the traditions, he grew dissatisfied and resigned his position on the board, and later on the worship committee. After the initial pleasantries today, I asked him point blank, "Am I the reason you resigned?"

"Well, I wouldn't put it that way," he said. "I quit because I didn't think things were being done in line with the quality of the way things were done in the past. I had considered resigning for a long time, and, to be quite honest, some of my disaffection predated you."

I'm sure there were things he didn't like about me that he didn't choose to tell, but I felt better, anyway.

The second man I visited was a fellow who had two heart attacks in the last year. I failed to visit him either time. I confessed to him the difficulty I have visiting people I don't know, and we both felt better.

September 16

Judith's doctor told me today that she is making substantial progress. He said that, depending on how she fares at home on Yom Kippur, he might be able to discharge her in the next couple of weeks. I was jubilant. Judith was pleased, too, and a little leery. She has adjusted to life in the hospital.

I went to a meeting of the Five Towns Coalition tonight, and I've had it. I've got to give up on this organization.

For the last eight months, we've had meeting after meeting in which we've tried to develop one project after another. And nothing seems to get done. Most of the time, nothing even gets begun. It's hopeless.

September 17

Judith has taken a turn for the worse; the doctor, the eternal optimist, calls it a "breakthrough."

One of her problems has been that she has never been able to show hostility, and now only through the therapy has she finally begun to learn how to be openly angry. The trouble is, according to the doctor, she doesn't yet know how to deal with her anger once she gets it out. Expressed emotions are so foreign to her they scare her out of her wits. This afternoon she was practically incoherent with emotion.

A certain amount of her new hostility has been directed

toward me. The doctor says she is really angry with herself for her inability to do things the way she would like to do them and, as a result, she is lashing out in frustration, as we all do, at those closest to her.

Her doctor also says that he doesn't feel I was at fault in her breakdown. He feels that the basic problem lies with her parents. They raised Judith by training her not to show emotions, and drilling her to hold it all in behind an icy aristocratic veneer.

Her parents are very detached people. Judith has now been seriously ill in the hospital for nearly a month, and they have not called her or me in weeks.

Instead, they have been mailing me weekly checks to help pay for the housekeeper, which they must think discharges them from all other obligations. It's frightful for Judith. Here is a woman with no friends who cannot even find friendship in her own family. I had to send her a New Year's card myself and sign their names to it. I couldn't bear to have her face the reality, that at a time like this, her parents were not thinking of her.

In the Bible, there is the story of the brothers Cain and Abel, both of whom bring equal offerings to God. For no obvious good reason, God accepts one and not the other. Cain, whose offering is rejected, grows angry and slays Abel. (Or is it Abel who slays Cain? I always get them confused.) In any case, the rabbis, in studying this Biblical passage, debated whether Cain (or Abel) had a right to be angry. They agreed he did. What he did not have a right to do was slay his brother. That was his crime.

In this context, I have always felt that I had a right to have all kinds of negative feelings from jealousies to hatreds, and I accept them without allowing them to frighten me. They are natural.

Well, I feel very hostile toward my in-laws. Perhaps I'm angry at the whole situation, and they are my most convenient target, but I think it's more than that. When Judith first grew seriously ill, I called them often to report her condition. But they never called me. Finally, I stopped calling them. And they still haven't called me. There is a silent hostility between us. Meanwhile, of course, Judith suffers.

September 18

This was the housekeeper's day off, and I had to take care of Sally.

I'm exhausted.

September 19

After services today, the organist told me that the former cantor was wondering why I hadn't called him.

September 20

Judith seemed slightly improved today. Her doctor said he will still allow her to come home tomorrow for Yom Kippur. Depending on how she reacts, he said, he may discharge her altogether in the next few weeks.

A few weeks ago a member of my congregation who was recently divorced asked me to perform his second wedding. He said he wanted to have it in a temple, so I called Temple Israel and asked if we could use their chapel. They said they would have to discuss it. A few days later, they called me back and said that we could rent the bride's room, which is basically a large closet, for $50. In addition, we would have to use their rabbi, and he would cost $50, too.

"This is silly," I said.

"I'm sorry," was their reply, "but those are our rules. And rules are rules."

What brings the incident to mind is a situation which indicates that a similar atmosphere may be developing in my own congregation.

By next summer, we will have our own new building equipped with facilities to hold wedding and bar mitzvah receptions. Last night I received a phone call from one of the few non-wealthy members of our congregation, a woman whose son will have a bar mitzvah later next year. She had been inquiring about renting a room in the new building for the bar mitzvah reception and she had been told that if she did, she would have to use a union caterer.

The woman could not afford a caterer and had intended to do her own cooking at home. But the new rules are explicit: anyone renting the hall must use a union caterer. The reason for this is that the caterer gives a percentage back to the temple.

The woman was very upset. She was crying over the phone.

"Don't worry," I told her. "I'll straighten things out. I'm sure we can make an exception in your case."

I called the president, but he was out of town. I then called the person in charge of scheduling these affairs.

"The woman simply wants to do her own cooking," I said. "She can't afford a union caterer. She's willing to pay for the room, and that should be enough."

"Rabbi, please," I was told, "don't get involved. We have to raise money. We have to have rules."

I could hardly believe what I was hearing. Is what I detest so much about Temple Israel beginning to happen right in my own congregation? With the new building, will the institution and its continuation become an end in itself?

Is everything from now on to be justified on the basis of the perpetuation of Temple Sinai?

September 21

This afternoon I brought Sally with me, and we picked up Judith at the hospital. Judith was dressed and waiting, excited to be leaving the hospital for the first time in nearly a month.

The ride home was pleasant, because I made a special effort this morning to wear Sally out. Judith was calm, composed and hopeful. This was her test, and she knew it, even though I'm sure the doctors hadn't told her.

Tonight was the holiest night of the year, Kol Nidre service. We had our traditional dinner before fasting, and went to the temporary temple together.

I could see Judith making a tremendous effort to keep herself together. She did.

September 22

This morning, during a break in the services, Judith and I went home to pick up Sally and bring her back for the children's service. While we were home, I insisted that Judith break her fast. She needed the strength, even though she was doing fine.

As soon as we got back to the temple, suddenly, out of nowhere, and for no apparent reason, Judith burst into tears, convulsive, uncontrollable tears. She couldn't help it. The moment she'd stop, she'd start all over again. "Mommy, please don't cry," Sally told her. "I'll give you a pill and you'll feel better."

That, of course, only distressed Judith more.

"Martin," she said, crying, "I'm feeling so many contradictory feelings. I'm so confused."

I tried to comfort her. "You'll feel better, darling. This will pass."

She finally quieted a little, and since I had to conduct a service for the older children, I asked Mrs. Brackman and Mrs. Mandel to watch over her. I was gone for about an hour, and when I returned I learned that the ladies had taken Judith home. She had broken down again.

Although quite upset myself, I conducted the afternoon portion of the Yom Kippur services. Afterward, a number of people came up to me and said it was the best service they ever attended. I don't remember a moment of it.

I rushed home, exhausted from prayer and fasting, and thanked Mrs. Brackman and Mrs. Mandel, who had remained with Judith all afternoon. Judith was complaining that mysterious things were happening in the house. She was unbelievably tense, and still crying erratically.

I drove her back to the hospital, realizing, perhaps for the first time, that her illness was long-term, that any hope of her being discharged from the hospital in the near future had vanished.

Later on, I wondered about the day. All this worship, all this ritual, and yet, here was Judith, worse when it was over than before it had begun.

September 23

The doctor's explanation: Judith, having been in the hospital for a month, had come to idealize our home, and when she finally came home, she found that there were problems there, too.

She is now back in intensive therapy. He said there is no chance, short of a miracle, that she will recover without many more months of hospital care.

September 24

The new confirmation class is very hostile toward me. Probably because they regard me as a proto-parent, they enjoy making themselves a discipline problem, and in today's session they spent a good amount of the time yelling and screaming and disrupting the class. Their intent was clearly to taunt me.

This is the same way last year's class began, and then after a couple of months, they became more civilized. If last year's pattern holds true, I will start out as the target for their aggression toward adults, but when they realize that I am making an effort to understand them—and in some instances, even agree with them—they will cool down.

But this has nothing to do with the larger problem. I am simply not reaching them. They spurn my approach with yawns. Their eyes are filled with shiny cars and trips to Europe and getting into the right college. They don't care to see things the way I do. Usually, they don't even care to listen. Confirmation, to them, is just something that has to be done for their parents' sake or one more reason to throw a party.

Last week I asked the students to write an essay on what they think of their family, their temple, their religion, and themselves.

One student wrote that he loved his family, his temple, his Judaism, and himself. "My dream in life," he added, "is to go to Yale."

I am contemplating giving up the confirmation class and having somebody else teach it.

September 25

Judith is having an awful setback. I was able to see her only briefly today, but she was hostile, unresponsive, and withdrawn.

To make matters worse, the insurance has run out. Now the bill for hospitalizing her falls on me. The cost is unbelievable: $100 a day with no end in sight.

On my way home from the hospital I crossed a bridge an
came to a toll booth. The toll was a dime. I didn't have it.

After lecturing me, the toll collector made me sign an IOU took my license number and finally let me pass.

I'm getting obsessed by the subject of money.

September 26

I got a call last night from a woman in California who until recently lived in this community.

"Rabbi," she said, "I just wanted to let you know how much I appreciate what you've done for me. I want you to know what a friend you've been."

A friend? The only dealing we ever had was when I helped her in a custody case.

This morning I heard from another friend, a neighbor. He sent me a New Year's card, just as he did last year. I don't know why. The street that separates us could be a hundred miles wide. And yet I know he considers himself a friend. If I died tomorrow, he would probably attend my funeral. In life, however, we communicate by sending New Year's cards across a hundred-mile-wide street.

He is not a bad person. He means well. Like so many other people around here, he thinks that to be good means to be active in righteous causes, or to offer to do good things, or to be nice to people when he sees them. I know a thousand carbon copies of him in this community. Every time I meet one of them on the street, or at a social occasion, he is always very solicitous and very concerned. *How are you? How is Sally? How is Judith and-if-there's-anything-I-can-do-please-let-me-know.*

And yet, except for once, I can't recall a single occasion when somebody has said to me, "Rabbi, can I take care of Sally for you today?" Or: "Rabbi, would you like to come to dinner?" Or: "Rabbi, when can I visit Judith?"

With the exception of Rabbi Goodman, the rabbi emeritus, who went more or less out of a sense of duty, only one other member of the congregation has visited Judith in the hospital. And worse, not a single officer of the congregation, my *employers,* has asked me, in light of the expense of Judith's illness, if some financial accommodation could be made to help me out. I suspect that a line assembly worker at General Motors would get more decent treatment in this respect.

What's the matter with these people? What kind of life are they living? Causes and business and activities and organizations turn them on, but what about people? Don't they care about people? Can't they care for one another? My God, how many times have I shared their joy and eased them through their sorrow? Has my door ever been closed? Haven't I always been the one to care when all they needed was someone to care?

And now I need them. My wife is in a mental institution getting worse every day, and all I can think about is all the agony she would be spared if a few people would show her that they care enough about her to make a small trip to the hospital. And yet all I get is *How are you—How is Sally—How is Judith?*

I'm sick and tired of being nothing more than a cardboard box that moves around. I can see what it's doing to me. I'm becoming as brutal as they are.

This morning I conducted the funeral of an eighty-year-old grandmother of a woman in the congregation. I didn't even visit the family. I called last night and asked about the grandmother over the telephone and then showed up this morning to perform the service with my glib professional words. Certainly a woman who lived for eighty years deserved more than that.

After the service, because it was damp outside, I decided not to go to the cemetery. I can't remember another funeral when I did not go to the cemetery.

What is happening to me?

September 28

It was a quiet day, the first in months. I didn't go to the hospital. I sent Sally out with the housekeeper.

I felt I had to be alone.

I needed the time to understand what has happened with Judith, but instead I ended up tormenting myself.

I convinced myself that I was the one responsible for getting her sick, because I have the largest of all responsibilities to her. I am her husband. And I took her for granted. I gave her strength, and then in neglecting her, allowed it to diminish.

I can't blame her parents. I can't blame this community. I can't blame Sally. I can only blame myself.

I caused her to get sick, by not appreciating her when she was well.

By evening, I had totally incapacitated myself with self-recrimination. I couldn't do anything to deal with the anguish.

I had no way to make apologies for myself, and nobody else to make them for me.

September 29

The board of trustees of Temple Sinai met tonight to ratify my contract. One person wanted the vacation provision clarified, and another bitched that the salary increase was too great, and in three minutes, the discussion was over.

And then the contract was approved unanimously.

Later

So it went. So it goes.

After eight months of intensive therapy, Judith was discharged from University Hospital on May 4, 1970.

She functions again—at a more restricted pace, of course. She is a changed person, so new that, at times, she stands back and looks at herself, and sometimes she is frightened by what she sees. Although old repressions have been lifted, she must puzzle out ways of dealing with the new facets of her personality.

She is not fully recovered, but she is trying. She is learning. She is marvelously determined to be strong and well again, this time for good.

More and more, I can see where I was at fault. She needed me, needed me desperately for all the reasons I raised throughout my diary, and I—I needed my causes. I needed my organizations.

All those meetings, all those groups, all those issues—I cannot help but feel now that so much of it was wasted effort, wasted time. We accomplished nothing of significance.

Unless people have a genuine feeling for each other, causes are pointless. They become substitutes for personal exchanges. People like myself, who wrap themselves in causes, find themselves working around—but rarely within—human relationships.

And human relationships, ultimately, are all that matter.

I learned this from my wife. While she was a good Jew to me, I was out trying to be a good Jew to the world.

How pretentious. How egotistical.

I can see, in my diary, pretention, egotism, selfishness, callousness, ambition, even hostility. I can see good points, too, but right now they do not fully compensate.

Like Judith, I am trying. I know I have to get better, too. In the past six months, I've made some small gestures to free myself of the restraints my job imposes, the restraints I myself impose. I gave up a few organizations and became considerably less active in others. I bought a pair of bellbottom slacks. I even smoked marijuana once, and although I felt relaxed, or high, or whatever it is, I doubt that I'll try it again very often, if at all. I still feel that religion can create its own highs.

There weren't many highs, I'll admit, during the year of my diary.

Why am I the Rabbi? Why do I continue?

I have to.

It's necessary for Judith's recovery. I don't want her to have to worry about me, worry about what I'm going to do. One of the things that troubled her last spring, before she got ill, was my growing disenchantment with my situation.

There are lesser reasons.

I have no place else to go.

If I were a druggist, I'd be worrying about the drugstore all the time. If I taught college, I'd end up playing the same game with a different set of rules.

Here, I can at least touch a few people.

My role is grossly imperfect, but it does allow me some freedom, some flexibility. I do not always have to compromise my integrity. Certainly, there are frustrations, but there are moments, moments when I feel I am achieving something at Temple Sinai, moments when I am reaching someone, moments when I am adding some little bit.

These are the reasons I stay.

Or are they only excuses?

—MARTIN SIEGEL
Woodmere, New York

About the Author

RABBI MARTIN SIEGEL, thirty-seven years old, was born in Brooklyn and educated at Cornell University's School of Industrial and Labor Relations and at Hebrew Union College in Cincinnati. He was ordained in 1960, served two years as a Marine chaplain at Camp Lejeune, North Carolina, then accepted a rabbinical position in Wheeling, West Virginia. In 1967 he became the rabbi of Temple Sinai, a Reform congregation in Lawrence, New York. A contributor to magazines ranging from *The Christian Century* to *Southern Baptist Review* to *Jewish Frontier*, Rabbi Siegel has also written *The Judaization of Christianity*, a forthcoming theological work. He lives in Woodmere, New York, with his wife, Judith, and their four-year-old daughter, Sally.

About the Editor

MEL ZIEGLER, twenty-five years old, was born in Scranton, Pennsylvania. He attended Penn State University and Columbia University's Graduate School of Journalism. A contributor to *New York* magazine, he worked for the Miami *Herald* before joining the staff of Maddick Manuscripts, Inc.